Lessons from the Mountain

Lessons from the Mountain

Learning to See Yourself Through God's Eyes

Laura Oheim

Published by Game Changer Publishing

Front cover photograph by Kurt Oheim

Paperback ISBN: 979-8-90158-012-7

Hardcover ISBN: 979-8-90158-013-4

Digital ISBN: 979-8-90158-014-1

GAME CHANGER
PUBLISHING
www.GameChangerPublishing.com

Advance Praise

"Laura skillfully weaves her love for God, family, people, music, the mountains, and all of nature into a wonderfully engaging and enlightening tapestry of thought-provoking devotions. You will be delighted by the little vignettes she shares at the beginning of each session. And the accompanying scriptures and questions for discussion and reflection pack a hefty punch as she drills down to the heart of the Gospel. The hymns and worship songs she adds solidify the teaching in one more dimension. You will be blessed and challenged by Laura's insight and charm, and in the end, you'll want to add her to your list of favorite people you haven't yet met. I wholeheartedly recommend this book!"

— Gwen Green, Participant in Laura's Bible Study

"Reading these weekly devotionals feels like sitting across from my wise and trusted friend, Laura. She not only knows Scripture deeply but also lives it out with authenticity and grace. With a powerful and unmistakable voice, Laura brings each subject to life through insight, creativity, and grounded faith. Her reflections are both Biblically rich and deeply personal, often drawing from the sacred spaces we both cherish—our beloved cabins in the Sangre De Cristo Range in New Mexico. I, too, have walked those paths, marveled at those views, and lingered in those places over many summers. Laura's words bring them—and the God who meets us there—into sharp, beautiful focus. More than a weekly study, this devotional inspires, challenges, and invites us to live with greater honesty while drawing ever closer to God."

— Kyle Boston, Fellow Cabin Owner

"In *Lessons from the Mountain,* Laura Oheim offers a devotional that is both thought-provoking and deeply practical. Each weekly reflection invites readers to see their own 'mountain experiences' through the lens of scripture, guided by probing questions and fresh insights. This journey is rich with wisdom, encouragement, and God's presence, making it a devotional you'll look forward to week after week."

— Carol Phillips, Participant in Laura's Weekly Bible Study

Some of life's richest lessons are discovered in stillness—by a stream, under a wide sky, or in the quiet of a mountain morning. *Lessons From the Mountain* invites you to slow down and meet God in those sacred spaces.

Blending scripture, reflection, song, and prayer, Laura helps those of us with weary hearts find rest and renewal in the presence of the Creator. Written for those who pour out for others yet long to be filled again, each page is a gentle reminder that the God who shaped the mountains also tends to your soul."

— **Justin Roberts, Lead Pastor of Pinnacle Community Church, Amarillo, Texas**

Step Deeper Into
the Lessons!

Scan the QR code to explore a gallery of photos that bring **each** lesson to life! Access heartfelt testimonials and fresh insights I'll be sharing in the weeks and months ahead. Keep checking back— there's always more to learn from the mountain!

LessonsFromTheMountain.com

Lessons from the Mountain

Learning to See Yourself Through God's Eyes

A Personal and/or Group Study

LAURA OHEIM

Foreword

To know Laura is to truly love her. Her unwavering faith and whole-hearted devotion to the Lord shine brightly in everything she does. Those who encounter her quickly recognize a woman of conviction, grace, and strength. Her life is marked not only by her unshakable trust in God's Word but also by her bold willingness to live it out with authenticity. Laura's love for people flows naturally from her love for Christ, and it inspires those around her to pursue a deeper, richer walk with Him. She carries the rare combination of a teacher's wisdom and an encourager's heart, always ready to guide, uplift, and remind others of God's faithfulness.

This book is a beautiful outpouring of Laura's heart and calling. In its pages, you will discover not just stories or lessons, but living testimony—truth shaped by her experiences, her reflections, and her time with God. Every chapter echoes her genuine passion for Christ and her desire to see others grow in Him. Whether through practical insights, gentle encouragement, or vivid metaphors drawn from her life, Laura's writing invites you into a journey that is both personal and transformative.

No matter where you are in your faith—whether you are taking your first steps with the Lord or seeking to go deeper into His presence—this book will meet you right where you are. It will inspire you to press closer to Christ, encourage you to trust Him more fully, and remind you that faith is not just a belief but a way of life. As you read, expect to be moved, uplifted, and challenged in the best way. This work is more than a book—it is a companion for your walk with God, one that will point you toward the joy, peace, and hope found only in Him.

—Lisa Blake
Executive Director
Leadership Amarillo & Canyon

Table of Contents

← THE INSPIRATION FOR *LESSONS FROM THE MOUNTAIN:*
  THE MOUNTAIN AND THE WORD!

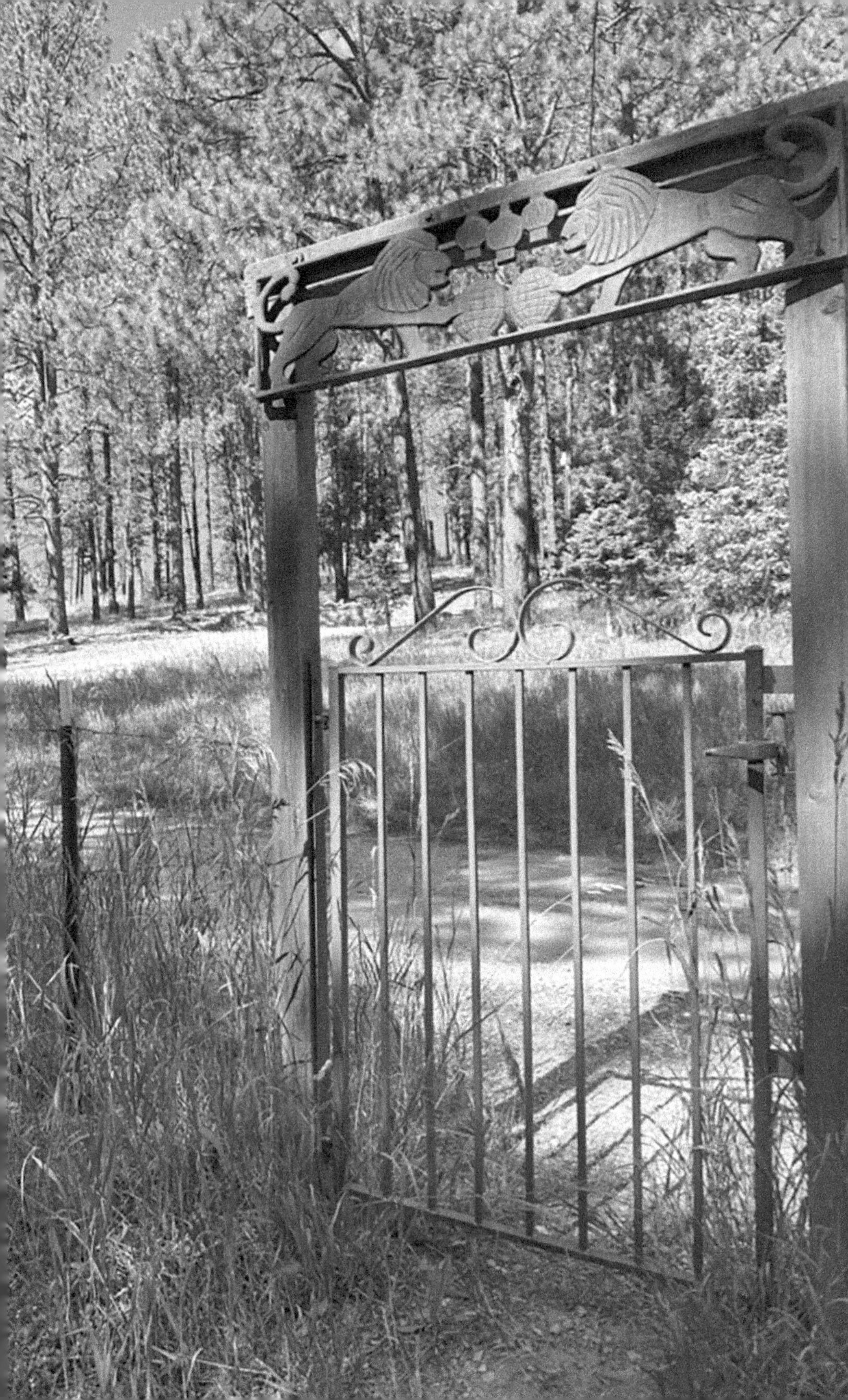

Introduction

I am writing this book for myself. Whether anyone else reads it, it has been purposeful in its writing. It's for me, but it might be for you, too. For those just starting out on their love journey with Jesus, this is for you. Right before our eyes, He places lessons we can learn by giving attention to His gift of creation. If anyone has spent their lives nurturing others, putting others' needs ahead of their own, taking care of families or loved ones, and hasn't stopped to recognize they are drained, or at least coming close to feeling empty, you may find it useful and meaningful. And for those who just love nature and what God can teach us through our observations, it might be for you, too. Whoever you are, and wherever you are on your Spiritual journey, I pray you find refreshment on these pages.

How to read these devotionals:

This book is *versatile*. It can be read as a personal devotional or used as a group study. This book is also *comprehensive*. It has many elements that can be used in a variety of ways, as described below:

1. Begin your time with a brief **prayer** of surrender, asking God to open your mind and heart to hear what He wants you to hear. Have a notebook in hand, ready to write your own thoughts or simply mark up these pages.

2. **Devotional:** Read and enjoy the devotional content, finding yourself in the story or one similar.

3. **Time in the Truth:** Spend time in the Word of God, choosing one or more of the Scriptures. Stay on one verse for as long as needed, and don't feel pressured to read them all. Most of the verses listed are also used in the discussion questions meant for either personal use or in a small group setting.

   Use any version you love, and read multiple versions to get the most clarity possible. There are also times when I suggest you read the verses in the Message version, MSG, in order to gain a better grasp of the Scripture.

4. **Mirror Moments:** Use these thoughts and questions to reflect on what was presented in the text AND from the Scriptures.

5. **Communion With My Creator:** Read my written prayer, but use it only as a launching point for yours. He longs to hear your heart and desires for you to share yourself with Him. This will be where God meets you.

6. **Song Suggestions:** Listen to the song or songs via YouTube or your favorite music streaming service if time allows. *The theme song for the entire project is "Creation Calls" by Brian Doerksen. Please consider listening and watching on YouTube before you even begin to read, as it captures the essence of the entire book!!*

7. **Themes** are provided and may be helpful in finding what fits best for you to read that day, but they are in no way comprehensive.

   Feel free to JUMP ALL OVER the book, as each chapter stands on its own!

8. **Discussion Questions** are provided for either further study on your own OR a group discussion with others, as this will deepen the lasting impression of each devotional. The Scripture verses used for group discussion mostly match with the verses suggested in **Time in the Truth**; however, there are some deviations.

9. Lastly, PLEASE use the **QR code** before or after reading each devotional that will take you to my website and provide a gallery of photos that bring each devotional to life, and more.

If you choose to enjoy these devotionals as a group, one of the benefits is that they all stand on their own. Therefore, if anyone must miss a gathering, they can easily come back and join right in. This also allows your group to pick and choose which lessons/topics you'd like to read for that week. Also, **please** feel free to pick and choose the Scriptures and questions that best serve the people in your group, as there are usually too many to cover in one sitting.

When I was a young girl at summer camp, about 11 or 12 years old, I sat by the stream and came up with simple word pictures of God's creation to go along with the truth of God I was beginning to understand for myself. I had a dream of sharing those "pictures" with others one day. I'm no longer 11 or 12. I've lived a lot of life and have, over time, refined those thoughts with the help of the experience life brings and the wisdom from my Heavenly Father. Ahead, you'll find some of those thoughts and others that I hope will bring some encouragement, possibly conviction, and hopefully refreshment to your hearts, minds, and souls.

There are 53 experiences tucked inside this book. You may choose to do them once a week or as often as your heart needs some encouragement. I hope you receive as much joy reading them as I have had writing them. Thank you for choosing to take a chance on *Lessons From the Mountain.* May God bless you and your journey.

BARBARA'S
BENCH

1. Barbara's Bench

A little bench sits tucked away under a big pine tree in our mountain community. It's a well-polished, hardwood, homemade bench that provides shade for all who stop to take a breath from hiking in the area. It not only provides a respite for hikers, a break from the sun, and just the right amount of space for you and a friend, but it also provides one of the best views of the valley below and the mountains climbing up behind. Although Barbara is no longer able to sit and admire the view, as I'm certain she has a better view from Heaven these days, the sign remains, and the bench is good for many years to come.

Do you have a Barbara's Bench? We all need one. We need to practice the important skill of stopping. Not just stopping, but Stopping, Stilling, Sitting, and Seeing. These four S's will allow our mental, emotional, and spiritual health to heal; to begin to restore what we may have lost in the rush of our lives; and to provide rest and rejuvenation to be filled for the future that is still ahead of us. We need to find "our bench" and do just that... Stop, Still, Sit, and See, so we can Rest, Refocus, Rejuvenate, and Refresh.

Now getting up to that beautiful, quaint bench takes work if you are hiking from anywhere lower on the mountain, which includes our cabin. There are ups, downs, rocks, and tree roots to traverse to get to the bench. So it's a worthwhile stopping place. There is the hard work and exertion of getting back to our cabin from Barbara's Bench as well. So, it's not a spot you find if you haven't lived some of life to get there, and it's not a staying spot either. It's simply a resting spot, one that is much needed and well deserved.

Consider the road you've been journeying. Does it have rough terrain, hurdles, slippery rocks, and tree roots? Then maybe it's time you find yourself a Barbara's Bench and sit for a while. Don't miss the shade it gives, the clarity it provides, the restoration for your tired body, and the blessing of the view!

← PHOTO TAKEN ON ONE OF MY MANY TRIPS TO BARBARA'S BENCH

Time in the Truth

- **Psalm 23:1-3**
- **Psalm 62:1-2**
- **Psalm 91:1-4**
- **Psalm 107:4-9**
- **John 16:33**

Mirror Moment

How has this journey we call life strained and/or drained you? Whatever it might be, could you experience restoration by seeking out your own Barbara's Bench and a much-needed stop? The journey from there will be refreshed for the next season of your life.

Communion with my Creator

Dearest Refresher of my Soul,

You are the everlasting Holy of Holies, and I exalt Your name above all others. You deserve my worship and praise for all that You are and all that You've done and all that You still must do in me and through me. I am grateful for the ways You have provided for me, given me blessings, and taught me lessons through the hard times.

I feel spent, used up, and tired. So, as I find my Barbara's Bench, I humbly stop, still, sit, and see that You are good! You are enough! I deeply desire to listen to Your direction and find Your presence in the silence.

And as I draw nearer to You, and in You, I will find the rest for my bones, the rejuvenation for my breath, and the refreshment You have for my soul.

In Jesus' name! Amen

Song Suggestions

Song Title	Artist
Restore My Soul	Vertical Worship
Be Still and Know	CeCe Winans
Still Waters	Leanna Crawford

Theme

Rest, Refocus, Restoration

Discussion Questions following *Barbara's Bench*

1. What troubles our spirits and hearts to the point of exhaustion? How does overthinking add to our exhaustion?

2. How have we dealt with these troubling things poorly in the past, and what are some ways we should deal with them in the future?

3. Do you have a Barbara's Bench? If so, what does your "stopping, stilling, sitting, and seeing" look like? And how might we learn to use our benches more effectively?

4. After reading **Psalm 23:1**, discuss what we NEED to do to have all we need. What are some "needs" we think we need?

5. What phrase stands out to you from **Psalm 62:1-2**, and why?

6. **Psalm 107:4-9** (MSG) Have you lived these verses? Where, in your life now, are YOU in these verses? I.e., staggering and stumbling, calling out to God, planting your feet, or thanking God?

7. Why did I say that Barbara's Bench is not a "staying spot"? What should happen in our lives after we've found and enjoyed our Bench?

8. **Prayer:** How did I start my prayer in the section Communion with the Creator? How does our perspective change when we first adore Him and thank Him?

9. To close your time together, pray and listen to one of the song suggestions listed.

2. Moo

On the way up to our cabin from the town below, there are meadows of green grass where, more times than not, a herd of cows is seen on one side of the road or the other. And sometimes they stand in the middle of the road, where you must just wait patiently until they choose to move. It's quite entertaining if you aren't in a hurry, and when you're on mountain time, you usually aren't. I pose the question, "What would you imagine these cows are doing most of the time?" I'm sure you guessed it if you've ever seen cows anywhere yourself. They are grazing. Their gaze is always directed downward in the grass. They are filling themselves full all day, every day. And if they aren't grazing, they are likely following another cow in a line, leading them to a better grazing spot or feed that has been spread for them.

Now, nothing against cows eating all day. I love a good hamburger and steak, and I think that is their created purpose. But if we compare what they are created to do versus what we are created to do, there should be a definite distinction and difference.

Yet sometimes we may look quite like a herd of cows, gazing downward, filling ourselves only to find the satisfaction is temporary at best. We aren't, or shouldn't be, bound by nature to gratify our stomachs or live for temporary pleasures.

Synonyms for "temporary" include "short-term," "passing," "brief," and even "makeshift." Compare these with the opposite: "lasting," "enduring," and "permanent." Wouldn't we all much rather live with an eternal mindset every day?!

We are meant for so much more than "short-lived." We are meant to keep our heads high above the pasture grass and make sure we aren't just following the leader to the next feeding trough. We were all created for the purpose of giving glory to God and bringing Him honor. We also have our individual callings that may even take us away from the herd and venture beyond the easy green pastures. That's the beginning of living, wouldn't you say?!

← PHOTO TAKEN BY ONE OF MY DEAREST FRIENDS, LISA BLAKE, WHO WAS HERE WITH HER FAMILY, AND WHO HAS ENCOURAGED ME THROUGHOUT THIS PROCESS!

Time in the Truth

- Mark 8:34-38
- Romans 6:12-14
- Jeremiah 29:11
- Ephesians 2:10
- Philippians 2:12-18
- Hebrews 12:1-3

Mirror Moment

Have you found yourself spending too much time grazing or following someone else or their "ideal" for you? Maybe it's time you evaluated your individual calling by asking, then risking, and fully trusting the Almighty Trustworthy God. Venture into the place He has picked out for you to become the person He originally designed you to be. Much more than a mooing cow! Think AND pray outside the box and LIVE BIG!

Communion with my Creator

Dear Almighty Purpose Giver,

First and foremost, You deserve my praise! All glory and honor belong only to You! I place You at the center of my being, instead of myself. I refuse to let my own desires come before Yours and lay down my own attempts to satisfy my needs. I offer You my weaknesses, my sorry attempts to find pleasure outside of Your will for me. For I know You have given me Your all. You have provided a way, by way of the suffering of the cross, to redeem me and make a way when I was blinded by my own way.

May my gaze be ever focused on You. Open my eyes to the wonderful purpose and calling You have created and designed specifically for me!

You are enough. You are my all in all. In You, I will find my satisfaction.

In Jesus' name! Amen

Song Suggestions

Song Title	Artist
Take Courage	Kristene DiMarco
Called Me Higher	All Sons and Daughters
Live Like That	Sidewalk Prophets

Theme
Purpose, Calling, Motivation, Courage

Discussion Questions following *Moo*

1. Do you believe God gives us each an individual calling? If so, have you discovered them? And if you feel led, please share to encourage others.

2. Was there a time when you felt an urge or calling of God but were afraid or felt incompetent to move forward in that calling, acting more like the cow that just keeps his or her head to the ground?

3. Jesus' own words in **Mark 8:34-38** are strong in nature. Read them and think carefully about what He says. What does He ask of us as His followers? Do these words excite you or frighten you? And what does He say will happen if we don't deny ourselves and follow Him? The world finds these words foolish and probably even scary, but as disciples of Christ, what emotions should this passage create?

4. God says to young Jeremiah in **Jeremiah 29:11**, "'I know the plans I have for you,' declares the Lord, 'plans for prosperity and not for disaster, to give you a future and a hope.'" Believe it or not, He has plans for you, too! Has your gaze been focused on what He has in store for you, no matter what stage or season of life you are in? During Jeremiah's life as a prophet, he was ridiculed much of the time, misunderstood, beaten, and imprisoned, but he continued to follow in the calling God had set before him. How does hardship in our calling often make us question it?

5. Read **Ephesians 2:10**. This verse has always convicted and humbled me to think God prepared good works for me to do for Him. Coupled with the many passages in *Psalms when the writers ask God to "establish my footsteps," "enlarge my steps under me," "turn my feet to Your testimonies," and "Your word is a lamp to my feet and a light to my path..." just to name a few. I know all I must do is ask for His guidance. I won't go wrong, even if the whole world disagrees. How might you interpret these verses as you discover God's plan for you and find the courage to move forward?

6. How does Paul in **Philippians 2:12-18** give us further instructions on how to obey and move forward in our work for God?

7. How does the success of our work, our calling, and our obedience to Christ look different from what the world deems as successful? This is a much-needed element to take into consideration when we try to measure "success."

8. Listen to the song suggestion, "Take Courage," or one of the others, and close by reading **Hebrews 12:1-3** as you courageously pray for God's direction and plan for your life.

*PSALM VERSES: **PSALM 119:133; 18:36; 119:105; 119:59**

3. Roots, Rocks, and Flowers

I've learned the hard way that even though the views up ahead are magnificent when hiking the mountain, you must look right ahead to ensure you'll stay upright. The roots and rocks that jut up from the ground need to be respected—or else. I've stumbled and fallen a few times when I was not aware of the next step ahead, and it shortened my hike.

We all love dreaming of the destination and concentrating on what we will do once we get there; however, the journey requires one step at a time. We must respect each step, regardless of how hard and sometimes treacherous we may find each one.

How often in life do we make grand plans without regard to the steps needed in order to get there and the unnecessary distractions we may encounter along the way? Maybe we don't consider the expense or toll it will take on us or those around us. Seeing the endgame is not a bad thing to do; it's a visionary move. However, the journey to get there, as I've learned over the years, is that we must also plan and expect for detours and pit stops, not being at all surprised at their appearance. Not treating them as inconveniences, but as lessons and even blessings. The joy should be found in the journey, not just the thrill of the finish line. If we know Jesus, then our final destination is quite settled. And what a relief and peace that brings as we pilgrimage this Earth.

But it's how we journey that should require our attention. Jesus is in our journey, and He's in the waiting as much as He's in and at the finish line. When we recognize the reality of these truths, we can take our time and face the detours or roadblocks with courage and perseverance.

I have gotten ahead of God many times in my own thoughts, ideas, and even my actions and words when it comes to "doing good" and producing what "I thought was rightly placed," only to find out I'd missed the opportunities of growth along the way, sometimes even to the point of damaging relationships.

Another benefit of stepping cautiously during those mountain hikes is the beautiful colors and shapes of rocks, the amazing root systems of the tall trees, and the colors and intricacies of the tiny flowers on the roadside. Our lives have these beauties as well, if only we allow ourselves to watch our steps, enjoy the journey, and embrace what He desires to show us along the way. For the lessons we learn during the journey will be priceless and just as beautiful as the finish line.

Time in the Truth

- **Deuteronomy 1:29-33**
- **Psalm 40:1-5**
- **Proverbs 4:24-27**
- **Psalm 18:31-36**
- **Psalm 119:100-105**
- **Proverbs 20:24**

Mirror Moment

Plans are important, and destinations are exciting! However, sticky notes and lists are just as necessary and valuable! Where do you need to slow down? What endgames you may already be playing out in your head need to be unrushed and unhurried? Deliberately find a pace where joy and patience exist one step at a time, and where God can teach you lessons in the roots, rocks, and flowers along the way! Be present.

Communion with my Creator

Dear Travel Companion,

Thank You that we have assurance of our eternity at home with You. You have created a way for us to be delivered and redeemed through Jesus' death and resurrection. My heart is forever grateful. I love to spend my days delighting in this reality.

But there are days ahead that need to be lived out. There is much to learn that You want to teach me, through the everyday ups and downs, hurdles, and ruts. You also have work for me to do for as long as I have breath in my lungs. Keep my eyes on You as I live today, and may my Heavenly mindset have the positive earthly effect You desire for me and those in my life.

In Jesus' name! Amen

Song Suggestions

Song Title	Artist
Joy in the Journey	Michael J. Card
Fix My Eyes	For King & Country

Theme

Focus, Direction, Goals, Distractions,

Waiting, Enjoying the Journey

Discussion Questions following *Roots, Rocks, and Flowers*

1. Along this road called life, have you found yourself skipping over lessons and blessings just to get to "your" finish line? How does preparing for a marathon, or a concert, or a big test have similarities to what we are discussing today? What are the things we can learn on the way to the finish line?

2. The verses recorded in **Deuteronomy 1** are a reminder of how God was ALWAYS with His people during the Exodus from Egypt to the Promised Land. In **verses 29-33**, He tells them AGAIN they don't need to fear because "the LORD Your God goes before you and will Himself fight for you..." After reading this text for yourself, discuss how we in our lives often forget this truth and what this can lead to. When we choose to live by the truth in these verses, how does it change our perspective?

3. **Psalm 40:1-5** is a beautiful picture of staying "in step" with God's plan. From 1) *understanding* the need to call on the Lord, then 2) *trusting* in the Lord, then 3) *waiting* on the Lord, and 4) *giving praise* to the Lord in the journey. Take a minute to reflect on a "journey" you've traveled and how you've either followed this path of wisdom, or not. What can you learn from this passage that could help you on a trek you find yourself on now?

4. Read the wisdom in **Proverbs 4:24-27** and discuss EACH directive and the positive effect they have on living this life. What traps do these instructions keep us from falling into?

5. Why do you think I named this devotional "Rocks, Roots, AND FLOWERS"? Why do you think I included flowers? I see flowers as the unexpected blessings we find among the distractions and pitfalls that come with living in our world. What blessings have you been witness to during hard seasons or just the daily grind of life? What blessings and wisdom do we gain from **Psalm 18:31-36** and **119:100-105** in our walk with God?

6. **Proverbs 20:24** says our steps are *ordered* and *ordained* by the Lord. Define "ordained." How does knowing your steps are ordained by the Almighty Sovereign God empower you to move forward and live your life?

7. Close by praying over each other's present journey and listening to one of the song suggestions listed.

4. Trash

It's a cardinal rule not to leave ANY trash outside or in your car in the mountains. Bears, raccoons, and other "curious" and hungry critters will find it and come back for more in the days ahead. In the case of the garbage, we must keep it inside the cabin until we are ready to put it in our vehicle and immediately take it to the sealed dumpsters. If this rule isn't adhered to, chaos ensues and comes back again to cause more damage.

In our lives, I feel certain we all have trash for which we are responsible. Don't worry, I'll be addressing the trash *others have put on us* in later devotionals. For now, let's focus on our own trash, something that, if you're like me, you rarely do. We have accumulated it and held onto it. From words we shouldn't have said, to judgments of others we shouldn't have made, to being critical when we should have been grateful, to placing expectations on others that were never agreed upon, to assumptions about others that were never fair, and the list goes on.

Keeping all that sealed up, in secret, hidden away without confessing and dealing with it, will ultimately make us stink as bad as the trash in my cabin. But bringing it into the light and positively dealing with it brings a breath of fresh air. Learning to treat this trash in such a way that we don't cause more harm to ourselves or others, and certainly not spread it so it causes more chaos in our lives, is paramount to our future peace. Not doing so only causes resentment, bitterness, and more anger to boil. We obviously don't have a garbage container we can drop this kind of trash in, but we have something even better. It may not be as easy as dumping trash into a dumpster, yet it's incredibly freeing when we have the courage to face it and deal correctly with it!

The path to taking care of our trash begins with confession to our Maker, surrendering our will and our ways to Him, and allowing healing to begin to take place. We have a loving Heavenly Father who is always readily available, allowing us to be honest with Him. Truthfully, we can't hide our trash from Him anyway, but He lets us hang on to it until we are ready to release it. And more times than not, a healthy step would be to find a trained professional counselor who can be trusted and confided in, where the pain is brought into the light, and we begin to address the next steps to healing relationships caused by our trash. Light exposes things in the darkness in order to bring freedom. Surrounding ourselves with a safe, sober-minded friend or friends to be sounding boards in the process is also a positive way of dealing with things from our past without keeping them stuffed away or spreading them further. All this so "bears" can't wreak havoc, spreading chaos with our undealt-with trash.

Admission of guilt leads to freedom. This lesson is NOT about shame. God is not a God of shame. Shame is the evil one's lie! Shame paralyzes us; but guilt can lead to confession, healing, and freedom. For more on the difference, see a trained professional!

Time in the Truth

- **Galatians 5:19-21**
- **Ephesians 4:29-31**
- **Colossians 3:5-9**
- **Psalm 51:1-12**
- **Psalm 139:23-24**
- **Isaiah 1:18-20**

- **Acts 3:19**
- **1 John 1:9, 10**
- **Galatians 5:22-24**
- **Ephesians 4:32**
- **Colossians 3:10-17**

Please refer to the questions in the study guide section to help you navigate reading these passages today.

Mirror Moment

What have you stuffed so far down that you can barely remember not feeling angry, resentful, bitter, and sad about? Don't let it continue to stink up your life, your thoughts, your reactions and responses, and steal your peace. Confess and surrender daily, followed by reading one or more of the Scriptures above to remind you how freeing it can be to your future!

Communion with my Creator

Dear Heavenly Healer of my Wrongdoings,

I believe You are Omniscient! I believe you are Omnipotent! I believe You are Omnipresent! You know all things. You are all Powerful. And You are everywhere simultaneously. These qualities of Your Being mystify me, thrill me, and yet they also terrify me. They terrify me, knowing that You know my deepest secrets, my hidden thoughts, and my wicked ways. Nowhere can I go from Your presence. In my flesh this truth is ominous, yet in my spirit and my soul, I am comforted and find rest in this truth. Nothing is hidden from You. Therefore, I confess to You openly and surrender my shame, guilt, sins, and myself. You are waiting and ready to offer me forgiveness, cleanse my stains, and embrace me. I am grateful, and I am humbled.

In Jesus' name! Amen

Song Suggestions

Song Title	Artist
I Surrender All	Hymn
I Surrender Lord	Hillsong Worship
The River	Brian Doerksen

Theme

Recognition of Guilt, Confession,

Surrender, Letting Go, Healing

Discussion Questions following *Trash*

1. Why is trash a good way to describe sin? (Sin is separation from God, not just the symptoms we commonly associate with sin.)

2. What lies does the enemy whisper to us about our "trash" and keeping it hidden? Hint: Shame vs. Guilt.

3. Examine the lists of sins in the following verses and then be totally honest with yourself about the ones you battle with. Remember, the beginning of confession is recognizing and naming where we have fallen short.

   Galatians 5:19-21
   Ephesians 4: 29-31
   Colossians 3: 5-9

   NOTE: Define any of the terms you may not be familiar with. You may find it helpful to read these passages in the MSG version as you take an inventory of where you find yourself.

4. Once you have spent time identifying the areas where you struggle, it's time to confess, surrender, and move in the direction of restoration. Read the next set of verses as part of this process:

   Psalm 139:23-24
   Isaiah 1:18-20
   Acts 3:19
   1 John 1:9,10

   God's mercy is always present when we are genuine in our admission. Our flesh with its passions has been crucified! Take time now to listen to one of the song suggestions as you contemplate what you have read and discussed thus far.

5. God is the author of forgiveness. It is His desire to restore us. He is the only One who can truly rejuvenate and regenerate us to a right standing with Him and with each other. The next set of verses, many of which come directly after the lists of offenses, are there offering hope, healing, freedom, and joy.

   Galatians 5:22-24
   Ephesians 4:32
   Colossians 3:10-17

6. Close by reading the Communion prayer *together*.

   Side Note: Today's content is very deep and may be hard and painful, yet so freeing if done with openness and honesty. Make a commitment to others in your group that everything shared will be kept in the strictest confidence. Also, some of the questions may require more time and more personal soul-searching.

5. The Fog

Mountain fog can be blinding and paralyzing. I suppose any fog can be, yet when on the mountain where there are twists, turns, and drop-offs, it seems fog can also be incredibly treacherous. Our cabin is located up above a beautiful lake and a small town. Many times, when I go out walking early in the morning, I witness the fog covering the area below, creeping up to where I am. I know without a doubt what is under that fog—the lake and the town. I've seen it, driven it, and experienced it. Yet the fog makes it impossible for me to see with my natural eye. I must imagine and remember what lies beneath. I know the town and the lake. They are beautiful. But you'd never know it when the fog sets in.

How good is your memory when the "fog" sets in? What keeps you from remembering the blessings or the goodness because of momentary distresses or maybe even a long season of blinding fog? Fog comes in all sorts of uninviting flavors. It comes in the way of loss, grief, sadness, depression, disease, physical pain, anger, fear, abuse, what feels like failure, confusion, and bitterness. It can come instantly or begin like a shifting shadow until it becomes all-encompassing and incapacitating. But whatever causes it, it is paralyzing. Stiff, rigid, immovable, drowning, stuck... Pick your word for what you are dealing with.

I'd like to offer a salve for your paralyzing fog. A Hope that won't disappoint. A Hope that is a wholehearted, evidence-based condition. The Hope that exists and is still with you, fighting for you, for your present and your future, even if you can't see it.

Find the mountain until the fog lifts! Look higher than your fog. I'm not saying it's easy. Sometimes it even feels "safer" within the haze, or you have no idea how to see beyond it. But getting lost in the fog only creates more confusion and chaos, and who truly wants that? The longer you linger in the mist, the harder it will be for your fog to lift. So, I suggest you find a place higher than the pain. Fix your eyes on Jesus and dare to be creative in the process! Keep your eyes focused on the One who will remind you of the beauty of the lake and the town that is there, who desires to be your refuge and your strength amidst your suffering. He wants you to steal away up to the mountain and find His presence. Rest in his comfort. Seek His direction. Listen for His voice. Follow His guidance and His clarity until the fog lifts and your eyes can once again see the beauty of the lake and the town.

Whatever confusion surrounds you, surround yourself with Jesus. Find respite on the mountaintop, looking up, trusting the One who is Trustworthy. He has proven it over and over again. Trust Him now.

Time in the Truth

- **Psalm 61**
- **Psalm 71:1-9**
  (read more of
  Psalm 71 for further
  encouragement)
- **Habakkuk 3:17-19**
- **Daniel 3:18**
- **Hebrews 13:15**

Mirror Moment

Where is your fog the densest? What feels blinding or paralyzing in your life at this moment? Could it be time to reach higher, knowing the Almighty is already waiting for you to call on Him? This may mean resting in His written Word or leaning on the Word Himself, Jesus, just to get you through the blindness. It might mean confessing, surrendering, and crying on His shoulder. Whatever it is, look higher, and be expectant!

Communion with my Creator

Dear Fog Clearer and Blue-Sky Reminder,

I bring You a sacrifice of praise today as I am struggling within this fog. Struggling with feeling lost in my hurt and sadness. Yet I still know You deserve my praise and all of my worship. Therefore, even in my present state, I adore and worship You!

As my body feels weary and my heart feels weak, I am reminded this is exactly when Your strength and power can work miracles in my life. I hold on tightly to Your goodness. I rise up to feel Your faithfulness. I remember what You've done in the past to protect, provide for, and restore my hurting soul. For these remembrances make my present bearable, and I will seek to stay above the fog and rejoice always!

To the One who always can, Amen

Song Suggestions

Song Title	Artist
Gratitude	Brandon Lake
Surrounded	Upperroom

Theme

Rising Above Your Circumstances, In the Waiting,

Feeling Stuck, Even If, Gratefulness

Discussion Questions following *The Fog*

1. Where have you experienced "fog" in your life? Past or present. How would you describe your feelings?

2. Many Psalms follow the same pattern of lament, calling out to God when their lives are unmanageable, seeking God in their distress. As examples, read both **Psalm 61 and 71**. Follow the path that the Psalmists take as they call out to God. How do they begin, what are their feelings at first, what do they remind themselves of, and how do they end their writings? Other Psalms that follow this same pattern are **Psalm 6, 10, 13, 22, 38, 42, 43, 69, 130**.

3. In great distress, Habakkuk implores God to intervene for the Israelites. He also tries to convince himself of God's goodness and faithfulness in the midst of the evil and tragedy in the world. He uses the same pattern of lament we see in many of the Psalms to lodge a complaint and then draws God's attention to the suffering, even stationing himself on the watchtower awaiting God's response. God responds, not with immediate relief, as we all hope He would do, then and now, but gives Habakkuk hope for the future, that one day he (and we) will see justice. Therefore, we are reminded that God is always faithful, and we should be as well. In **Habakkuk 3:17-19** we read Habakkuk's final words. How might his words encourage us? In several Bible translations, what are the first two words Habakkuk speaks?

4. Discuss the situation surrounding what occurs in Daniel 3. Then read **Daniel 3:18** and take note of the "even if" in this verse. How hard is that to say and to live by? So, if the fog never seems to lift, what carries us through?

5. Write your own Psalm or lament, being very detailed with how you feel and what can be gained from looking to Him for comfort, guidance, strength, a new perspective and outlook, hope, and peace.

    A lament includes the following:
    a. Address God,
    b. Complaint,
    c. Confess your trust in God,
    d. Petition or request,
    e. Praise and express trust in God's sovereignty

6. Close your time together by using the prayer provided, **Hebrews 13:15**, and listen to one of the song suggestions.

6. At the Gate, Turn Left

I had a couple of friends visit "my mountain." I always love it when I can share this treasure with those I love! They were staying at a cabin below mine but fairly close to a beautiful meadow, so I gave them directions as to how to find this hidden gem! I specifically said go through the gate by the outdoor chapel and turn left. Follow the road, and it will take you to the meadow and the beautiful scenery surrounding it.

Anxious to set out and being sure they knew the way, they misinterpreted "turn left" to mean "turn right." After turning right and walking a bit, they soon became perplexed when they encountered a fork in the road instead of the beautiful green grass and brook. When they inquired and even sent a picture of where they found themselves, I immediately knew what had caused this confusion. The lack of precision. "Turn left" had become "Turn right!" My simple direction once I saw the photo was, "Turn around." With only a small disruption, they turned around, walked back past the gate, and soon found the meadow, filled with beautiful mountain grasses, wildflowers, a babbling brook, and mountains towering all around!

This simple mistake reminds me of how often I have not taken the time to listen to God's direction and calling for my life. *Listening* should be a top priority instead of being one step or more ahead of the One who knows the way I should go. *Listening* to the voice of the Holy Spirit and His accuracy for detail.

Setting off on my own path, thinking I know full well which way to go has gotten me caught in snares of my own making, with the full intention of wanting to please God, but not gathering the wisdom needed to journey on ahead. After setting off on **my** course, I usually recognize my mistake(s), present God with my "picture" (just like my friends did for me), and He makes it clear I didn't take the time to get my "assignment," even if it was just a matter of left or right.

You see, over the years, taking into consideration my "quick to move ahead" would have been better if I'd instead "been quick to slow down, *listen,* and remember" that direction and precision matter! The One True God is a God of order and of detail.

This is also true even if I don't like what that direction or precision is. I've realized obedience and trust is a much better plan than my own.

I know for certain my friends *wanted* to listen and follow my directions; they just got ahead of me. Over the years, I've gotten ahead of God, the cart before the horse thing. I'd like to help you avoid those mistakes and wait for clear directions. Then follow them slowly, one step at a time. And if the answer isn't clear, be persistent in your asking, and remember, let Him set the pace and the path. Our lives are a marathon set on His map, not a sprint mapped out on our own.

Time in the Truth

- **Proverbs 3:5, 6; 5:21-23; 16:9; 19:21; 20:24**
- **James 4:13-15**
- **Isaiah 55:6-9**
- **1 Corinthians 13:12**

Listening and hearing from God:
- **Psalms 23:1; 62:5;**
- **1 Chronicles 16:11;**
- **Luke 6:12;**
- **John 10:27-29; 14:26:**
- **Romans 8:26, 27;**
- **Ecclesiastes 7:5**

Mirror Moment

Where are you ahead of God's plan? Wanting to get to the solution quickly will cause us to jump ahead. Where is precision in God's communication to you not being heeded? Listening, for those of us who like to talk... well, it just doesn't come easily, but it is paramount in knowing the right direction. Then, obedience, with His exact, perfect timing, is the answer to our anxious thoughts and our longing to find the beauty of the meadow. Slow down, as I've mentioned in previous devotionals, but it bears repeating, to take the time to ask for wisdom and then, and only then, pick up your "marching orders" and take a step.

Communion with my Creator

Dear Director of my Direction,

I often get ahead of You. More times than not, I act first before I pray for direction. And even when I ask, I don't always stop to truly listen. Thank You for never giving up on me, even when I do things my way. Make me aware of where I am ahead of

You. Draw me back to You first, and then to the plans You have for me: guiding me and strengthening me as I follow You!

In Jesus' name! Amen

Song Suggestions

Song Title	Artist
Trust and Obey	Big Daddy Weave
Thy Will Be Done	Hillary Scott
I Will Follow	Chris Tomlin

Theme
Details, Direction, Accuracy, Getting Lost, Obedience

Discussion Questions following *At the Gate, Turn Left*

1. How likely are you to follow a map (GPS these days) OR use your "instincts" to find where you're going? Do you like landmarks or directional words to help you?

2. Jumping right into what happens when we put our own plans in front of God's and get caught in snares, read **Proverbs 5:21-23**. What is the caution spoken here for going about doing things our own way? Move to **Proverbs 16:9** and ask yourself how often your own way has gotten in the way of His plan for you. Be willing to share personal experiences that may help others.

3. I love the way **Proverbs 20:24** says plainly we are lost and wandering without God's guidance. What are your thoughts? How do **Proverbs 19:21** and **James 4:13-15** remind us we are not in control of anything? Does this message bring comfort to you or frighten you? How does **Proverbs 3:5-8** summarize beautifully how we are supposed to live, and the benefits reaped from trusting Him?

4. Beyond the wisdom gleaned from these verses, what does **Isaiah 55:6-9** remind us is still possible when we find ourselves lost or having veered off the path we should be on? What does He offer us, and what comfort can be found in this passage?

5. **1 Corinthians 13:12** makes it apparent that we aren't supposed to see clearly in this life. Knowing this, discuss how we should move forward if we can't see clearly. Clues can be found in **1 Kings 2:3** and all through **Psalm 119**!

6. One of the problems my friends had in stepping out to find the meadow I described was their lack of listening to the details of the directions. It was a silly mistake and one that was quickly remedied. However, I personally tend to lack the necessary listening skills when it matters more. On the occasions where I have stopped to listen, the detours and distractions were kept to a minimum. *Listening* is a skill and a practice that unfortunately often comes AFTER we've tried other methods or plans, if at all. Read some of the following verses about listening and hearing from God. Discuss how we can be better listeners, and discover the benefits of listening for guidance.

   Psalm 23;
   Psalm 62:5;
   1 Chronicles 16:11;
   Luke 6:12;
   John 10:27-29;
   John 14:26;
   Romans 8:26-27;
   Ecclesiastes 7:5

7. There are so many voices out there. Distinguishing between the right Voice and the noise, as well as listening to that Voice, are paramount to our obedience. Discuss the voices in the world and then spend time sharing what listening requires? Time permitting, share when you heard a clear message from God.

8. Find a rendition of the old hymn "Trust and Obey," my suggestion would be Big Daddy Weave. Listen prayerfully. Use this as a closure to today's study and your own personal prayer as you begin discerning God's voice of direction. The other song suggestions are also powerful and can be listened to as well.

7. What Makes the Grass Grow?

One summer when my husband and I came up to the cabin, we decided to plant some grass seed in hopes that it would grow and make our space more beautiful. One day, we worked all day breaking up the ground and sprinkling the seeds, then covering them again in hopes the seed would soon show what it was created to do! My hubby said, "Be generous with the seed," so I threw what seemed like tons of seed into the well-tilled ground. That was all we could do—be generous with the seeds and wait.

It was actually up to the rain and the sun, provided by God, that would actually do the "trick" and produce the "miracle" called growth! To our amazement that evening, the rains came, and they came hard and long and constant for 24 hours. We had no idea how fast the seeds would actually produce, and yet within only a couple of days we could see tiny shoots with the sun and rain that continued. The grass was hardy that season.

As amazing as this illustration is, this hasn't always been the norm in my life when it comes to planting seeds of goodness and grace to others. Quite the opposite, or so my limited vision has shown. On many occasions I've planted seeds and been overly generous with the seeds, just like in our front yard, only to be disappointed in the "short-term outcome." I have been discouraged and exhausted, having shown compassion, kindness, hours of mentoring, and praying. All to find, in my limited view, only a "field of dirt" in response. Yet over the years I have learned a lesson worth noting. That is, I'm not in charge of what becomes of those seeds. I'm only called to plant them generously and nurture them to my ability, with God's help and energy. It's up to the soil they've been planted in, the receptiveness of the ground, and the nutrients of the sun and rain to make those seeds grow—none of which I have any control over.

← THIS IS *NOT* A PHOTO OF OUR FRONT YARD... HOWEVER, IT IS A PHOTO OF A MEADOW NOT FAR FROM OUR CABIN WE WALK BY ALMOST DAILY ON OUR WALKS.

Have you ever "planted seeds" in people's lives and expected them to grow instantly, or at least within our line of sight and in a "reasonable" amount of time? It doesn't work that way though, much to our chagrin. The truth is, we are asked to be the messengers, the **generous** seed throwers, and even the cheerleaders, and then leave the growth and development to the only One who can help us all to grow.

I've had to release and let go of so much inner turmoil over the years when I didn't see the fruits of the labor I thought was good and positively planted. Releasing and letting go has been freeing, knowing I was faithful with what was required and asked of me. Have you felt the same? Then surrender the control and hurt and continue to plant generously!

Time in the Truth

- **Luke 6:35-38**
- **Acts 20:35**
- **2 Corinthians 9:6,7**
- **James 2:8-10;12-17**
- **Hebrews 13:16**
- **1 Peter 5:6,7 (MSG)**
- **Galatians 6:9,10 (MSG)**

Mirror Moment

Being ground tillers and seed throwers is our main purpose on Earth other than loving God with our whole hearts. Yet, we often get discouraged if, when we tirelessly till and throw, "we" don't see results on our timeline, with our limited eyesight. Even writing this makes me think what an overly pompous person I am sometimes. Who do I think I am? Everything we do should be for His glory, and the mere fact that we are allowed to be His hands and feet, tilling and throwing His seeds at all, should bring me to my knees in grateful praise. So instead of you getting a Mirror Moment for yourself today, you got my personal one. And just maybe you can relate.

Communion with my Creator

Dear Seed, Plant, Flower, and Tree Grower,

Only You, dear Father, can make the trees and flowers grow! And only You, dear Spirit, can make our fellow humans bloom into Your potential for their lives! Make me a generous ground tiller and seed thrower, and let me watch You do the rest! And if I don't see it, help me to release all control over it, knowing I've done exactly what You've called me to do, for YOUR GLORY!

In Jesus' name! Amen

Song Suggestion

Song Title	Artist
Trust in You	Lauren Daigle

Theme

Planting Seeds, Being Kind No Matter What,

Control, Letting God Do the Growing

Discussion Questions following *What Makes the Grass Grow?*

1. Do you consider yourself to have a green thumb or not when it comes to plants? If you have a green thumb, enlighten the group on what some of your tips are!

2. This question is actually a many-layered question. Take time to read and think through each one! What does planting seeds for God look like in the life of a Jesus follower? How has your life been impacted by a person who planted seeds in your life? How has your seed planting impacted others that you've witnessed? Are there cases where your seed scattering has "seemed" to do no good? What lessons have you learned or can you learn from this?

3. Phew... That was a long discussion question... Hopefully it brought to light some of the truly great things that have happened when you've offered God's light and truth to others, and I'm sure it also brought up some frustrations in sharing God's Word. In light of what you've just discussed, read the following passages to gain some much-needed encouragement, boldness, courage, and comfort. Spend some time discussing 1) How God knows and recognizes our efforts, 2) How God imparts the wisdom we need when we honor Him whether others see it or not, and 3) How we are NOT in control of the outcomes.

   Luke 6:35-38 (MSG)
   Acts 20:35
   2 Corinthians 9:6, 7 This may be referring to finances, but I believe it can also speak to the giving of much more (time, resources, emotional outpouring)
   James 2:8-10;12-17
   Hebrews 13:16

4. I'd like us to consider a word that came up in a couple of the previous passages: *sacrifice*. We are called to sacrifice. Not an easy or comfortable concept in our culture. Nevertheless, a necessary one in God's economy. Explore the word "sacrifice" and discuss how sacrifice when we are spreading seeds of God's grace and truth comes into play. We have the greatest example of sacrifice in God's sacrifice of His Son. How can that truth bring us back to a place of humility?

5. Our last exploration today will cover a topic I personally need to continue to learn. Completely embracing that I AM NOT IN CONTROL OF ANYTHING! GOD IS! No matter how many seeds I scatter... no matter how many lives I've invested in... no matter how many Bible verses I've shared... no matter how many long hours I've spent loving on others on behalf of God's kingdom, I AM NOT IN CONTROL OF THE OUTCOME! When I finally recognized, realized, and embraced this truth, there was and is freedom! Read **1 Peter 5:6,7** (MSG) and **Galatians 6:9,10** (MSG), knowing He sees what you've done and will continue to do if you don't lose hope. He's where the HOPE is, and He is all that matters!

6. Pray together and listen to Lauren Daigle's song "Trust in You" as you close.

8. The View

From our deck we have a gorgeous view of a myriad of different species of pine trees, an aspen grove, mountain ridges, peaks above the tree line, and a beautiful sky above. I never get enough of this view. I can sit all day, every day, and still want more. No photo does it justice, even though I try often! It is amazingly peaceful, restful, refreshing, and comforting. Whether the weather is bright sunshine, partly cloudy, gray cloudy, hazy, foggy, rainy, or even snowy, I never can get enough of the view. And it's no surprise that no day's view is quite the same. I'm mesmerized by it. Each season is filled with beauty. It's the same, only different. From bright yellows to the green shades of trees to the orange and pink sky of the setting sun, it's like a refreshment for my eyes!

You'll hear me talk A LOT about our view, but hopefully each time with a different twist on lessons I've learned. So please bear with me every time I bring it up.

Similarly to this ever-changing yet perfectly stationary frame of a view, I see and experience God's Word. His truth is never changing, His character is never faltering, and His love is never failing. However, it offers powerful strength to each situation, revealing life-sustaining messages, all depending on what I need at the moment. It is meant to be solid and "rock worthy," yet bending to provide exactly what my life needs at that moment.

Have you ever read a passage one day, received one message, and discovered that in the next reading of the same verses there is different wisdom to embrace? Maybe you're focusing on one word of the passage one day and another word the next. The Holy Spirit has a way of making all things new. And because ALL Scripture is inspired by God, it can speak to our every need! No two photos of the mountain are exactly alike; no two readings are the same. God is the absolute best artist ever, and as I gaze upon the landscape, I am incredibly humbled to see a glimpse of that from our deck. And the Holy Spirit through Scripture is a beautiful artist we all have the opportunity to experience if we allow it to be!

Time in the Truth

- **2 Timothy 3:16**
- **Psalm 19**

Mirror Moment

Do you get tired of "your view," otherwise known as your life at this moment? Maybe try seeing it from God's perspective. Ask the Holy Spirit to open the eyes of your heart and for new lenses to see what He is doing to draw you to Him. If He's asking you to do the hard thing so the view will get better, He will absolutely provide the way.

If He's asking you to be patient where you are right now, rest in His Truth, knowing He's in the waiting. And if you find yourself floundering in the dark, in uncharted waters, find the Light of His Word and lean in until the day dawns brighter and the storm passes. Whatever His message, be reassured He hasn't left you. He's given you a chance to see the changing seasons and appreciate each one!

Communion with my Creator

Dear Author and Artist of All,

Your canvas amazes me! I'm thankful for all the colors of the rainbow. I thank You for allowing me to see this beauty from earthly eyes! I am a witness to Your amazing creation, AND I am a part of it! As I marvel at the different hues, let me also marvel when I read the Truth from Your Word, as it brings color and life to every aspect of my being! The varying tints, tones, and tinges that each reading of the Scripture brings make me want more and bring You praise forevermore!

In Jesus' name! Amen

Song Suggestions

Song Title	Artist
Great is Thy Faithfulness	Traditional Hymn
Forever	Kari Jobe
Word of God Speak	Mercy Me

Theme

The Bible, God's Word, and His Truth Never Changes

Discussion Questions following *The View*

1. Besides the Bible, what is a favorite book you've read and the impact it's had on your life?

2. The Bible is the inspired Word of God. Read **2 Timothy 3:16** and discuss its power in your life. Scholars have argued over time about the inerrancy and the infallibility of Scripture. If you have time, study these words and their definitions as they are attached to Scripture. For me, and what I personally believe, God's Word is infallible, and with the help of the Holy Spirit, I can and will and have gleaned exactly what God has for me every time I open my Bible.

3. Though there are many "contributors," the Bible is the authoritative Word of God. If you feel comfortable with your group, please share what verses have spoken to you. Take as much time to share as you need, knowing that the verses you share will likely touch others! Let this be the "meat" of your gathering today.

4. **Psalm 19** is the perfect chapter to study in bringing together the beauty of God's Earth and His written Word. God, through David, expressed just how God writes His glory in the Heavens as well as in Scripture! Go verse by verse and make the comparisons. See how marvelously God works to weave His creation with this treasure trove and love story called the Bible.

5. The Communion with the Creator and any of the songs suggested in this devotional will be a wonderful way to bring your lesson to a close today.

   To add to your discussion and for deeper study, you'll find additional information on understanding and interpreting Scripture on the next page.

Understanding and Interpreting Scripture

I. The Reliability & Authority of Scripture

Scripture is God-inspired (God-breathed). It is not our ideas about God; it is God's revelation about who He is and about our identity in Him.

2 Timothy 3:16 (NASB) "All Scripture is inspired by God and beneficial for teaching, for rebuke, for correction, for training in righteousness."

- **Inerrant** – Refers to the original texts as being without error.

- **Infallible** – Refers to the current text/translation; when interpreted with submission to the Holy Spirit it will never fail to guide or lead us in God's will and plan for our lives.

II. Reading *and* "Hearing" Scripture

Matthew 7:26 (NET) "Everyone who hears these words of mine and does not do them is like a foolish man who built his house on sand."

Romans 10:17 (NASB) "So faith comes from hearing, and hearing by the word of Christ."

III. Understanding Scripture

- **Exegesis** – Reading God's will and meaning *out of* the text.

- **Eisegesis** – Reading our limited and misguided presuppositions *into* the text.

It is better to ask: *What is Scripture telling us?* rather than *What do I think this text is saying?*

Understanding Scripture requires considering context and allowing Scripture to interpret Scripture. The context of Scripture arises from an **Eastern cultural framework**, not a Western one.

Eastern Cultures	Western Cultures
Live in **Kairos Time** (quality time)	Live in **Kronos Time** (clock time)
Contemplative	Utilitarian
Seeks the "why"	Seeks the "how"
Simplicity	Complexity
Cherishes wisdom learned	Cherishes new ideas
People as community	People as individuals

IV. Three Approaches to Biblical Translation

1. **Literal Translation** (word-for-word)
   KJV, NASB, ESV, NET

2. **Dynamic Equivalent** (thought-for-thought)
   NIV, NLT, Amplified, NET

3. **Free Translation (paraphrases)**
   Living Bible, Phillips, The Message

9. Be Prepared

I carry a whistle and a foghorn! That's right. Every time I venture out on our mountain, I don't leave home without those two necessary pieces of "equipment." Why? Because of the bear sightings all over our mountain. I have never seen a bear on the mountain personally, yet I have seen the pictures, and I have had neighbors call to me from the safety of their homes while I'm out walking to be careful because they've just spotted a bear roaming their property. Oh yes—and then there was the bear my husband saw looking out our front window during the middle of the night on our deck!

Do I believe these sightings to be real? Absolutely. Therefore, I prepare. I'm actually not certain what a foghorn sound or a whistle would do for the ominous bear, but I am fairly confident it would give me time, at least to escape. Better than even my preparation against a bear attack is my certainty of being prepared against the evil one, alive and well, who lurks in order to steal, destroy, and kill those of us who are following Jesus every day. This very real threat requires our preparation. It requires us to take seriously what can happen if we let Satan attempt to get a foothold or even toehold into our personal space as we carry on throughout our day. Satan doesn't come dressed as a little red demon with a pitchfork, or even a black bear. He is sly, dressed as light, and much harder to recognize. But he is lurking, and he is real. That is why we MUST be prepared.

If we aren't prepared and we haven't adequately placed on our armor, fully equipping ourselves with the protection of His covering, we are extremely likely to be injured at the least and destroyed at most. Don't wait until it's too late. Admit your vulnerabilities and limitations and stay prepared.

Time in the Truth

- **John 10:10**
- **Isaiah 41:10**
- **Ephesians 6:10-20**
- **Colossians 1:13, 14**
- **Colossians 3:2**
- **1 Peter 2:9,10**
- **1 John 5:19, 20**

← OUR COMMUNITY HAS WEEKLY SUMMER SERVICES AND
ONE OF OUR DEAR RESIDENTS BUILT THIS PULPIT.

Mirror Moment

Consider how you get ready each day. You brush your teeth, drink your coffee, dress, apply makeup... Those are all fine and good; however, the best way to prepare for each day is to grab your foghorn and whistle—translated, your armor of God! Read, study, and pray before you begin your day. **Ephesians 6:10-20** will help prepare for each day!

Communion with my Creator

Oh Holy and Perfect Armor Constructor,

Dress me, Lord, today and every day. I know my real enemy is the Devil. I know the battles I fight within myself and with others are spiritual ones that can only be fought with Your protection. Make me mindful every morning when I prepare for my day of how important it is to be strong in Your might in order to be able to stand firm against the evil one. Whatever the evil's disguise, give me discernment to recognize it and call on Your Holy Name to vanquish him!

I give You the glory and honor and praise beforehand for how You will protect and provide.

In Jesus' name! Amen

Song Suggestions

Song Title	Artist
Warrior	Hannah Kerr
See A Victory	Elevation Worship

Theme

Preparation Against the Enemy

Discussion Questions following *Be Prepared*

1. On a light note, before we dig in, are you a planner or one who does things on the spur of the moment without much notice? If you're a planner, what does that look like? Or if you are a "spur of the moment" person what does that look like?

2. Read **John 10:10**. How should the *realization* and *reminder* that there is a real enemy cause us to respond? Take a bit more time in **John 10** as Jesus tells His apostles He is their shepherd. What stands out to you as you consider this beautiful analogy? Key phrases: His voice, robbers and thieves, the door...

3. Are you naturally a fearful person? How has that helped or harmed you? Recognizing danger can produce fear in us. **Isaiah 41:10** speaks to fear. What are the comforting and strengthening words spoken by Isaiah to the Israelites and to us today that can dispel that fear, but keep us *vigilant* against evil?

4. **Ephesians 6:10-20** is a perfect illustration of how to be prepared against the evil one. Pour over the parts of the Armor of God and how each part of this metaphor relates to our being prepared and protected as a believer against the attacks. Get specific!

5. How does truth in the following verses continue to encourage us along our journey where the devil prowls? And what examples of these truths have you seen in your own life!?

   Colossians 1:13,14
   Colossians 3:2
   1 Peter 2:9,10
   1 John 5:19, 20

6) Pray either your own prayer or the one written, and listen to one of the powerful songs suggested as you close your time together.

10. Memories Matter

I had the delightful chance to meet the grown grandson of one of the first caretakers for our mountain community! Let me back up a bit so you understand my delight in being the one who got to meet him and hear his story. Our mountain community has a caretaker who watches out for all the cabins and helps when there is a need for our cabin owners. This person is very important to our community and becomes highly appreciated as they do their job well. A particular caretaker, who was extremely valued, was Mayme Marrs. Her husband had been the caretaker in the earliest of days, the 1930s, and on his passing, she took his place and became the beloved Mayme that everyone still talks about. Our Chapel and Community Center were even named for her as a memorial after her passing. This all happened long before our time on the mountain. But from what I understand, she was a "pistol packin' mama" and wasn't afraid to use it either. She killed raccoons in the trees as they attempted to destroy them, and threatened to shoot the vagrants who would come and stay uninvited on the property of others! Quite the character for sure. A real Wild West "she-sheriff."

Jump ahead to 2022. I found myself in the caretaker's cabin on some other business, and a man came knocking on the door. To my surprise, it was Mayme's grandson and his wife from South Carolina, just "driving through," he said, and he hadn't been there in thirty years. He immediately began telling me about his grandmother and the amazing memories he had of spending summers there with her when he was a child. He drew a vivid picture of what the land had looked like, what the earliest cabins were like, where there'd been a little bridge over the stream, and where he and his grandmother used to sit under the trees for long periods of time and, in his words, "just be." It was definitely a walk down memory lane. He became a little boy in those few moments we had together. The light in his eyes and the excited expressions as he talked gave me pause to consider the importance of memory. This gentleman hadn't been to the mountain in decades, but it was like he'd never left when he began "drawing" for me and his wife the picture from his memories.

Memories matter, both good and bad, for different reasons. There are places for both types of memories. Memories can be powerful, and they deserve our attention today. They should be brought to mind often, not to dwell on the past, but so they can keep us humble and grateful and also bring us hope!

I find that we often race through life, forgetting the importance of every moment God gives us to live. Or at least not stopping to reminisce about the things we've learned, the people we've known, the lives we've touched, and the love of others. The gift of moments God so graciously showers on us that should be and need to be remembered. Here's to a healthy dose of reflecting and becoming a little girl or boy for a short while.

Time in the Truth

- **Genesis 9:14-16**
- **Deuteronomy 4:9;10; 4:23,24; 6:12; 8:10-20**
- **1 Chronicles 16:8-19**
- **Psalm 77:11-15**
- **Psalm 103:1-5**
- **Isaiah 46:8,9**
- **1 Corinthians 11:24,25**
- **John 14:26,27**
- **Numbers 15:37-41**

Mirror Moment

Choose a memory today that you hadn't thought about in a very long time—one that has God's fingerprints all over it. Something that brings joy and a smile to your face. Because memories matter, they bring hope and courage to seasons that are void of happy, joyful moments. They remind us of God's provision and love that are waiting to be remembered and new ones to come.

Communion with my Creator

Dear Memory Maker,

As I sit with You today, Father, I am grateful for our minds. Minds that can recollect memories. Those that bring joy to my soul and a smile to my face, as well as painful ones where I've learned lessons and felt Your comforting Presence. May I always remember all that You've done for me. Your grace and mercy, Your goodness and love, and Your faithfulness and gentleness. Keep ever present in my mind the sacrifice of your Son and the resurrection power, which reminds us of who we are and whose we are! I give You ALL my praise!

In Jesus' name! Amen

Song Suggestion

Song Title	Artist
Remember	Lauren Daigle

Theme

The Power of Remembering, Memories, Recollecting

Discussion Questions following *Memories Matter*

1. What is one of your happiest childhood memories? How does remembering this occasion make you feel, and why is it important today to remember it?

2. God has a very high regard for remembering. **Genesis 9:14-16** is one of the earliest times when God asks the people to remember, and we still see this amazing promise today. Now check out the following verses in Deuteronomy, where God was reminding the Israelites not to forget everything He had done for them. How do these verses relate to our own lives? **Deuteronomy 4:9,10; 4:23, 24; 6:12; 8:10-20** What can happen in times of plenty and satisfaction?

3. **1 Chronicles 16:8-19** is reminding the Israelites to "remember His wonderful deeds which He has done..." What are some of the wonderful deeds He has done in your life? And where have you seen God's Fingerprints on your life? Include the miracles you've seen happen!

4. Read the following verses with a keen eye for what the listeners are asked to remember, and why is this so important?

   Psalm 77:11-15 (The title for this Psalm is "Comfort in Trouble from Recalling God's Mighty Deeds"!)
   Psalm 103:1-5
   Isaiah 46:8, 9

5. All Scripture is given to us so we won't forget the Lord our God! The Gospels, written by three apostles, Matthew, Mark (Peter's gospel), John, and Luke (a doctor who interviewed eyewitnesses of Jesus' life), were written down so we would NOT forget the life of Jesus, from birth to death! *Memory is that important.* What story of Jesus resonates with you, and why? Consider Jesus' birth story, or His parables, or the miracles He performed. How should these truths and remembering them impact our lives today and in the future?

6. What are we still asked to do regularly as Jesus followers so we don't forget the sacrifice of His son? Hint: **1 Corinthians 11:24, 25**. Why should Communion be held in such high regard in all Christian churches?

7. One of the Holy Spirit's functions in our lives is to bring to mind all we've learned about God. In **John 14:26, 27**, John reminds us of this truth. How has the Holy Spirit brought to mind the truth we need to hear?

8. To end your time today, read Numbers **15:37-41**. The Israelites were being asked to remember God and all He had done for them. How can a physical reminder help us to remember? Consider sharing a tassel or other physical reminder that will do just that! Close in prayer and the song suggestion.

11. The Lost Art of Waving

Taking time to visit neighbors, slowing down long enough to wave, sharing a smile, being kind, and considering others more valuable than yourself seem to have gotten lost in the crazy world we live in.

The flip side, which we see too often today, is passing without speaking, acting "put out" when others are "in our space," rushing through life without lifting our heads from our phones, speeding towards red lights, and always looking out for number one.

I think I'd rather go back to the days of waving! On the mountain, it's a REAL thing. The waves are genuine, the "hello's" and "how are you's" are sincere, the invitations to "sit for a while" are authentic... for most folks anyway :).

What does it take to be kind? It takes a small amount of time, a bit of getting out of our comfort zone, a lifted hand, a kind word, a bit of risk, and a raised head from our own selfish behavior. And what are the benefits, you might ask: a returned smile, new friendships, and depth of relationships. However, even if those don't come, we've been faithful to show the love and kindness God created in us to display. The "cup runneth over" kind of kindness. Our cup will be fuller. We will see the world from a half-full perspective, maybe even fuller than half, rather than a half-empty one. Try it out today, and you'll be surprised that the one to reap the rewards will likely be you!

P.S. I recently had the opportunity to help with a meal at our church for a family who had lost a loved one. We do this whenever there is a loss, to show our love and support. There were several of us serving, and as we worked alongside one another, I was struck by the way serving is a perfect way to reap the rewards of this life and deepen friendships. Being a blessing to this family and sharing God's gifts of our time and a comforting meal made their grief a little easier and certainly enriched our lives. This is only one example of the multiple ways we can take "waving" to our neighbors to an even higher level.

Side note and a word of caution: If waving causes fear due to abuse or an unsafe feeling on your part, please refrain. This simple devotional in no way wants anyone to be put in harm's way or cause additional trauma to someone who discerns danger.

Time in the Truth

- **Galatians 5:22-25**
- **Philippians 2:1-8**
- **Philemon 1:4-7**

Mirror Moment

When paying it forward, doing the right thing, sharing a smile, or waving—even when it feels awkward—becomes your norm, something beautiful happens. You begin to plant seeds of kindness in others and brighten their days, whether they tell you or not. In turn, your life becomes more enriched, full, and flourishing. And at the end of the day, the blessing will be yours. Be a waver!

Communion with my Creator

Dear Filler of my Cup,

You are the true Filler of my cup! And just as You've filled my cup, make me a cup filler as well. A waver and a smiler. A gentler, kinder person when the opposite tries to trick me into being unkind or uninterested. Stop me long enough to acknowledge the one who has been left behind or the one who needs a pick-me-up. Thank you, Father, for reminding me that mountaintop wavers and friends belong and are needed in the valley as well!

In Jesus' name! Amen

Song Suggestion

Song Title	Artist
Kindness	Chris Tomlin

Theme
Neighborly, Being Kind

Discussion Questions following *The Lost Art of Waving*

1. When you are out in the world, do you look people in the eye and smile, or do you keep your head down and move forward? No condemnation here, just a bit of self-awareness.

2. Have you ever taken the time to go out of your way to smile and strike up a conversation? If so, what became of that encounter?

3. **Galatians 5:22-25** in Scripture is referred to as the "Fruit of the Spirit." Read these verses together and discuss the qualities we should possess as Jesus followers. How does the act of waving, smiling, and being aware of your surroundings become a witness of the love of God to others? When have you possibly fallen short of this simple act of sharing Jesus?

4. Christ came to show us how to live! His life should always be what we imitate! The powerful words of Paul in **Philippians 2:1-8** remind us of how Jesus lived, and therefore, how we should also live every day. Take time to unpack this set of verses, considering Jesus' humility and His way of relating to others. What can we glean from Him in our interaction with everyone we meet?

5. Consider the kindness you've shared with those who are less than kind to you. At the end of the day, what did you take away from this act of love? On the flip side, perhaps consider when you've been less kind to those who have been less than kind to you. What impact has that had on you?

6. I'd like to be remembered as a modern-day Philemon! He obviously was doing the work of God when Paul called him a beloved brother and fellow worker! Read **Philemon 1:4-7**. How do these words of encouragement spur Philemon on to continue the cause of Christ? How do words of encouragement spur you on to be a better version of yourself?

7. What does a wave and a smile cost us? How can these actions be used by God to bring about change for those we encounter? When have they been game changers for you as well?

8. If you feel your cup isn't full enough to share a smile or wave, ask God to be the "filler of your cup"! In closing, read the Communion prayer, listen to the song suggestion, and claim the wealth of His nourishment so you are able to be a waver wherever you are!

12. Cattle Guards

Driving over the cattle guards coming and going from our mountain to town is a constant reminder of their importance for the cattle that roam in the grassy fields surrounding our beautiful space. If the cattle were to get through the fences or outside the safety of the cattle guard, their fate would be sealed, and they likely wouldn't survive for long.

Cattle guards to human relational boundaries translates easily. A life without boundaries is doomed to be chaotic and much like riding a roller coaster of jerks, twists, turns, high speed, fits, starts... repeat. Unhealthy relationships thrive on "unboundaried" lives. Anger, resentment, expectations, confusion, frustrations, and the like are all products of living without healthy boundaries. Not an appealing way to live, but sadly, where many of us DO live.

Our boundaries must be set for the purpose of our own sanity, as well as that of others. Caution before any further discussion here: Don't let others set boundaries for you, and also, don't allow anyone to belittle you into thinking you aren't worthy of boundaries.

Boundaries are quite a simple concept and can make all the difference in bringing peace and order into your world. This lesson was learned recently in my life when I had expectations I felt were reasonable, when I thought I knew what was best, without taking into consideration how others were affected. So, the lessons I learned from having healthy boundaries for myself and respecting others' boundaries for themselves have made clear where I end and they begin and vice versa. As painful as this process can be, with open self-examination, self-discovery, self-control, and honesty with yourself, it usually proves to be well worth it.

It takes practicing what we preach as Jesus followers: recognition, admission, confession, and forgiveness. Not all outcomes look the same; some may result in restored relationships, whereas others, if toxic and detrimental in nature, may not. However, both will free you and bring a new vibrancy to your life!

I'd highly suggest that you investigate for yourself if you've placed healthy boundaries in your life and relationships. You'll find, like I did, a wonderful new freedom to walk in because you were brave enough to do so.

Time in the Truth

- **Proverbs 4:23**
- **Proverbs 22:3,4**
- **Matthew 18:15-20**

- **Galatians 6:1-5**
- **James 5:16**
- **1 John 1:9**

Mirror Moment

Where are you in need of healthy boundaries in your relationships? Do you find that either you or others overstep into each other's lives, crowding who you are or demanding too much from you, or vice versa? Do you have expectations or assumptions of others, or even yourself, that they, or you, can't live up to? Is someone being too dependent on you? Maybe it's a friend, or an adult child, or even your spouse. Get the book *Boundaries* by Dr. Henry Cloud and find the help you need there. It was transformational to me. I hope it will be for you as well.

Communion with my Creator

Dear Original Boundary Maker,

Sometimes, I find myself always wanting to fix things and think I know what's best for others. I am consciously handing over the control I've had for long enough, knowing You are the only one who truly knows what they need and how to help them, as well as what I need. This mess I've made for myself by blurring the lines of where I end and others begin, and vice versa, can only be solved with Your sovereign help. I openly confess and surrender where I've tried to be God. You alone can and will help me as I move forward one day at a time, as You work to untangle the web that was never supposed to be woven.

I've also been hurt by others' need to control me. God, give me the courage to stand up and draw lines so they no longer keep me from thriving.

Giving You all the praise beforehand for the masterpiece You want to create in me!

In Jesus' name! Amen

Song Suggestions

Song Title	Artist
Boundary Lines	Chris Tomlin
Make Room	Community Music

Theme

Need for Boundaries

Discussion Questions following *Cattle Guard*

1. When you are out in the world, do you look people in 1) What emotions are stirred when you think of boundaries, and why?

   Do you agree with the statement in the second paragraph of the devotional that reads, "A life without boundaries is doomed..."?

   And how would you finish the statement if you do agree?

2. Consider the following questions, discussing each one, before diving into Scripture.

   a. How does having *control* in our relationships affect our view of boundaries? Where might *surrender* and *forgiveness* fit into this picture?

   b. Where has a lack of boundaries in your life caused *pain*? Where has setting healthy boundaries in your life brought about the *peace* you need to live in good relationships?

   c. Why do some people resist or view boundaries as negative?

   d. Has someone placed a boundary around themselves that seems unfair to you?

3. **Proverbs 4:23** What does protecting your heart have to do with setting boundaries?

4. **Proverbs 22:3, 4** What are the differences between the two types of people described in these verses, and how does healthy boundary setting fit in?

5. **Matthew 18:15-20** is Jesus' perfect picture of dealing with earthly relationships. How does wisdom from God serve us well in setting boundaries?

6. **Galatians 6:1-5 (MSG)** What actions are expressed in this passage that can be beneficial in our plan to set boundaries?

7. **James 5:16** Consider how not setting boundaries has potentially harmed your relationships. What steps can be taken, using this verse, to make things right?

8. The prayer today focuses on the act of confessing. Stop long enough to add your own confession as you strive to build and strengthen God's ideal for the healthiest relationships. Listening to the song suggestions can also add insight into healthy boundary setting.

13. Angel's Attic

There is a store where I love to shop that thrives from its many donors and customers, located at the bottom of our mountain in the small community below. It's important to note it's only open Thursday-Saturday from 10:00 a.m. to 2:00 p.m. I always plan around my other activities so I can make sure to go early and beat the rush! Of all things, it's a thrift store, full of people's odds and ends and discards. As is very true, "One man's junk is another's treasure." Oh, so true, especially when it comes to Angel's Attic, in my humble opinion.

We've stocked much of our cabin with goodies found from there—dishes, sheets, towels, etc. We've also taken many items there to be sold. And the best thing about the store is that all the workers are volunteers and members of a local church, AND every penny collected goes toward countless Christian missions proudly displayed on signs in the store. The good goes around and around and blesses everyone.

Now I hardly ever leave empty-handed, always proudly walking out with either a necessity for the cabin or a little something fun I've chosen that "I can't live without"! The treasure hunt begins as I walk through the door and ends with "triumph" as I leave. It's my kind of fun.

What does this have to do with our lives? I liken it to searching for the good hidden inside everyone. If we walk into a meeting, a store, a conference, a classroom, a church, a study, a family gathering, or anywhere that people meet, we should begin a treasure hunt. One that will certainly end in leaving triumphantly because it's how we were created to be! A hunt that will look past the blemishes, the hurts, the anger, and the sadness and find the treasure hidden away inside each person we encounter. This may take some practice. Some of the practices may include looking past facial expressions coming from the other person, putting old grudges aside, offering forgiveness, and giving second chances. Most importantly, it's seeing people through the lens of Jesus, with His compassion, His grace, and His mercy. We may leave the gathering some days with many treasures in our hearts and others with only the hope that we'll have another chance to discover treasures we've missed. But don't leave discouraged. Leave knowing you did what, as Jesus' followers, we were created to do, and that is to show love.

Side Note: I would like to add that this does NOT include people who are unsafe for you. It also doesn't mean you should be a doormat so others can constantly belittle and walk all over you. Jesus' example shows that he loved, but He also showed justice and spoke the truth when needed!

When it comes to difficult people, ask for God's wisdom to see things the way He does and act likewise.

Time in the Truth

- **Philippians 2:1-8**
- **Colossians 3:1-17**
- **2 Thessalonians 3:16**
- **Hebrews 13:1, 2**

Mirror Moment

Jesus hunted "treasures..." us! He certainly did it when he donned His earthly cloak, and since we are to use His example as to the way to live our own, let's go treasure hunting whenever possible. It should lower our frustrations, anger, and resentment, and it's certain to bring more joy into our lives.

Communion with my Creator

To the Ultimate Treasure Hunter,

You pursued me and showed me a better way. You sought me, and I surrendered to Your love. I am justified, sanctified, and made new because of Your search for me. So, it's my turn to treasure hunt and find the best in everyone I encounter, showing them Your love. Make me an instrument of your making, playing only the song you have for me to play. May my song point to You in all I say and do.

In Jesus' name! Amen

Song Suggestions

Song Title	Artist
If We Are the Body	Casting Crowns
Give Me Your Eyes	Brandon Heath
Love Them Like Jesus	Casting Crowns
Not in a Hurry	United Pursuit

Theme

Searching for and Recognizing the Good in Everyone

Discussion Questions following *Angel's Attic*

1. Do you like thrift store shopping? If so, what do you often like to buy there? And if you don't, why not?

2. Have you ever encountered difficult people? I'm sure we probably all answered this in the affirmative. How does our human side want us to react when we do?

3. In **Philippians 2:1-8**, we are asked to have the "same mind" and the "same attitude" as Christ. From these verses and other qualities of God that we know of Him, what does this mean for us? How challenging is this charge? And why?

4. **Colossians 3:1-17** reiterates how we are to live.

   a. We usually skip over, or at least gloss over, the evil practices of our old self listed at the beginning of this chapter. Spend time on the lists in **verses 5, 8, and 9** wrestling and confessing what areas you still struggle with.

   b. What should we do when we've identified the areas we battle with? How can **verses 10 and 11** help to answer that question?

   c. Using the remainder of this passage, what is the mandate given to us on how to live towards others, OR "treasure hunt"?

5. The MSG version of **2 Thessalonians 3:16** says, "May the Master of Peace Himself give you the gift of getting along with each other at all times, in all ways. May the Master be truly among you!"

    How does knowing the Master is "truly among us" make it possible to find the good in others?

6. Stop now and listen to one or more of the song suggestions. How do the songs shift our perspective when interacting with those who are hard to see positively? What are some of the lines for the songs you've chosen to listen to that speak to you directly?

7. Because we live in a fallen world, there will be people who we attempt to find the good in that are so unhealthy they are unsafe to be around. If you have the time and feel comfortable sharing, discuss what that has looked like in your life.

8. Finally, as you close this discussion, spend time in prayer. Pray Christ will teach you how to love like He does, feel what He feels, and see what He sees! And go treasure hunting today and every day!

14. Bats

Growing up a city girl, I only saw bats around Halloween, and they were portrayed with witches and spiderwebs, and frankly, I wasn't a fan. And I certainly never saw a real bat. All of that was long before I watched how they are perfectly timed, and perfectly positioned, to do what they were created to do! Eat annoying bugs and mosquitoes! And who could call that scary? I call it genius!

At dusk, if you sit in a recliner on the mountain watching the sky, bats fill the air, flitting overhead and taking care of business. I've grown to thoroughly enjoy watching them and being reminded of God's order in the Universe.

Everything we see within creation has its job, its purpose. Look around and find the purposes of God's creation. Some examples are the amazing sun that is perfectly placed to bring heat without burning us up; the moon to reflect the sun, giving light in the darkness; the pull upon the earth so we will stay grounded; growing vegetation that provides food for us and oxygen for us to breathe; and trees towering to provide nests for birds and then perhaps one day being used to make lumber or paper.

This is a ridiculously short list, but be proactive today in seeing the order God has for everything in creation! And don't forget, you are His creation; therefore, you have a place in the order as well! Find purpose for yourself, be aware of the purpose others have, and embrace both.

Time in the Truth

- **Genesis 1**
- **Ecclesiastes 3:1-11**

Mirror Moment

Take yourself outside today. Find a part of nature you hadn't thought of before now, or that you have overlooked, that holds a place in the order of God. Give Him thanks for reminding you that everything was created by Him, for a purpose and for His glory!

Communion with my Creator

Oh God, the God of Order,

There is complete order to Your creation, as well as complex unity within it. With You, and only with You, there is proper functioning. We read of the unity, completeness, and harmony in the Garden of Eden before that fateful day when humankind chose to do things their way. We often choose our way, and the outcomes are full of chaos, as was the choice of Adam and Eve. Your order and structure bring me hope. The circle of life with animals and seasons and all of creation reminds me that You also want order for me and for my life, for we are Your design as well! All of Your handiwork has order when it is directed and orchestrated by You! When I am distressed about the chaos ensuing around me or the disarray of thoughts in my own head, show me Your stability and bring me to the place where order is my norm, and there is no room for any other way to live my life.

In Jesus' name! Amen

Song Suggestions

Song Title	Artist
Creation Calls	Brian Doerksen *(Theme song for the entire book)* Consider watching the video along with listening. It can be found on YouTube.
So Will I	Hillsong United

Theme

Order and Purpose of the Universe

Discussion Questions following *Bats*

1. What is a part of nature that surprises you? Or makes you laugh?

2. Do you see yourself as an organized person? Discuss how order and organization keep our lives from chaos. Are there times when order and organization may not be a good idea? Share your thoughts.

3. Have you ever stopped to consider the complete order of our Universe and given God praise for it? Do that now! Start by listening to one of the song suggestions.

4. To further give God praise for His orderliness, read **Genesis 1**, stopping after each day's work to discuss how each part of His creation is an element of His design and plan!

5. Think about the variations of plants and trees and the diverse types of animals. Discuss God's creativity and purpose in all of it. What are some of the most interesting animals you can think of?

6. On a very different, yet important note, I've known people who struggle with chaos in their own minds, mainly due to trauma or mental challenges. Please know that is NOT God's design for you! Just like His extreme detail in all of His creation, He created your brain to function similarly, certainly not all jumbled up in confusion and disarray due to pain from others or a chemical imbalance. Our thought lives can wreak havoc on our ability to function and even see beauty in our world. God wants healing to occur and bring clarity and peace into your life. If this is you or someone you know, I encourage you to ask your friends to pray over you and to help find you a Christian therapist and/or a doctor to bring about restoration and soundness to your mind which is God's desire for you.

7. Read **Ecclesiastes 3:1-11**. Why do you think God placed this passage in Scripture? How do these verses remind us of God's plan and design for our lives?

8. Close today with a prayer of thanksgiving for His handiwork.

15. 9,000 Feet

Being born and raised in a city that is twenty-five feet BELOW sea level, moving to a tiny mountaintop town, where our cabin is almost at 9,000 feet ABOVE sea level, is quite a jump! It is a major adaptation for the body, especially the lungs! And when we talk about lungs, we have to talk about breathing! Breathing is, needless to say, essential to living, and if you've ever gone from one extreme to the other quickly, there is quite a difference and an adjustment.

In the mountains, you have to concentrate as your body adjusts to the lack of oxygen. You must pace yourself and rest accordingly until your body acclimates and breathing becomes easier once again. Just like breathing and the need for oxygen, is your need for Jesus and a relationship with Him. Without it, we face life on Earth with no foundation. When we only use our limited power, strength, and stamina, which surely give out, the result is gasping for air and taking everything and everyone down with us. Not the ending any of us wants.

Our conversation with Him should be as natural as breathing. But at any time if it isn't, we must get back to focusing on communing with Him, just like focusing on taking in enough air to sustain us when we are on the mountain. The lack of oxygen in our lungs can be likened to the places in our lives where we don't take Jesus. The recognition of our lack of oxygen and the time it takes to recover is much like our recognition of how much we need Jesus. Now, if we are believers, He is always with us, but the Spirit only comes alive in us if we give Him the reins and allow Him to release His power in and through us. We do this by turning our thoughts toward Him in the midst of doing ALL we do in our everyday lives, until it becomes as natural as breathing!

Start with something like, "Good morning, Lord. This is the day You have made, and I will rejoice in it!" End the day with something like, "Thank You for this day. You've allowed me to live, with all the blessings and the challenges that came my way. And help me to follow You better tomorrow."

← THIS PHOTO WAS TAKEN ON A HIKE A COUPLE OF FRIENDS AND I WERE ON. WHEN I SAW THIS CROSS, I KNEW IT NEEDED TO BE HIGHLIGHTED WHEN IT CAME TO DISCUSSING THE HEIGHTS!

This may seem extremely oversimplified, yet how often do we forget to begin and end our day with Him? I am speaking to myself as much as to each of you as I write this. And even when we do remember, some days will be harder to speak these simple phrases due to the challenges life puts before us. But if we commit to begin to proclaim them and speak the truth over our days, asking for guidance in the morning and thanking Him at the end of each one, we will see even the blessings when the air is very thin.

Time in the Truth

- **Philippians 4:8**
- **Psalms 51:7-12**
- **Isaiah 40:28-31**
- **2 Corinthians 10:3-5**
- **Ephesians 6:18**
- **1 Thessalonians 5:17**

Mirror Moment

What does the in-between look like? The in-between waking and sleeping?

How can your day be an open conversation, talking to and listening for Him? What about your thought life? Does it conform to the pattern of the world or of Christ?

Recognizing His presence, tapping into His strength, asking for His protection, and living deeply in His love and relationship is His greatest desire for us.

Try it. It won't disappoint.

Communion with my Creator

Dear Breath Giver,

May my every breath be a prayer!

I love You, Lord! I need You, Father! I trust You! Create a right spirit within me! Change my attitude where it needs to be changed! Let me always rejoice in Your faithfulness! Give me Your understanding! Make me more like You! Strengthen me for this challenge! I desire to depend only on You! Give me a hunger for Your Word! I want more of You, Lord!

Let my every breath be a prayer.

In Jesus' name! Amen

Song Suggestion

Song Title	Artist
Breathe	Michael W. Smith
There Is None Like You	Lenny LeBlanc

Theme
Our Need for Jesus, Our Thought Life

Discussion Questions following *9,000 Feet*

1. Has anyone ever experienced a time when it was hard to breathe, or you felt you didn't have the oxygen you needed? If so, how did it feel?

2. How does the need for oxygen translate to our need for Jesus?

3. Read **Psalms 51:7-12**. When we are deprived of what we need (oxygen and Jesus), we recognize we MUST make a change. How do these verses speak to the change we MUST make in order to inhale and exhale again? (Reminder: This Psalm was written after Nathan visited David and confronted him about his sin with Bathsheba; for further reference, see **2 Samuel 11**.)

4. After reading **Isaiah 40:28-31**, discuss this question. When our "oxygen" doesn't come at the time we would like, what can these truths provide for us in the waiting? And what part do we play in creating the atmosphere needed to receive that oxygen?

5. Read **2 Corinthians 10:3-5**. What are we asked to do in **verse 5?** How will doing this change the course of our day/life? What is released because of our obedience? Refer again to **verse 4**. Consider checking out this set of verses in the MSG version. What new insights might you gain?

6. **Ephesians 6:18** completes a prominent set of verses. Previous to this verse, the pieces of armor are described that we must put on daily to fight the battle against the enemy. Paul concludes by telling us to pray AT ALL TIMES in the Spirit! What does "praying in the Spirit" mean, and how can we make sure we do this daily?

7. **1 Thessalonians 5:17** This verse is tucked into a list of things as believers we must do for and with one another. In closing to this devotional, I believe it is the key to how we can tap into the oxygen available to us at 9,000 feet and above in our lives.

8. If you haven't already listened to the song suggestions, do so as your group closes its time together.

16. Rivers, Brooks, and Waterfalls

If you were to ask me what my favorite sound in all the world is, anyone who knows me well would say, "the sound of water"—the sound of waterfalls, waves crashing on a beach, rushing river water spilling over rocks and heading swiftly to the bigger waters below, and even the light, babbling sounds of the brooks that push slowly to join up with other tributaries downstream. Water sounds refresh my tired heart. And observing "moving" water restores hope to my soul.

Water provides cleansing, and it also represents life.

There is so much I could say about water and how it urges me forward and how it stays long etched in my sound bank when I need it most. What can I say, and how can I make you feel the way I do? Interestingly enough, in a small group I led years ago, I once asked the question, "What sound do you love most?" Besides the sounds of babies' laughter, water sounds took a resounding lead! So maybe you already feel the same way about water sounds as I do.

The power of water is used throughout the Scriptures, from the great Flood (showing great justice done) to the parting of the Red Sea (power against the world's greatest force at the time and redemption for His oppressed people) to the Woman at the Well (Jesus offering His Living Water) to Jesus using water to wash the disciples' feet (showing complete humility and compassion). Each and every one of these events commands our attention! There are so many good lessons to learn from each one!

For today's lesson, I will focus on the symbol of water as a cleansing agent. Who doesn't enjoy a shower after working outside in the heat of the day, or feel refreshed just by washing their hands after going to the playground with the kids, or replenish their body by drinking an icy cold glass of water after running a race?

God used water most powerfully in baptism to symbolize the cleansing from sin into rightness with Him. The washing away of the old and the squeaky clean of the new! You and I, we have that squeaky new clean if we've asked Jesus to cleanse us and restore us to union with Him. However, I have witnessed too many times fellow Jesus followers forgetting to live in their new reality and their new identity. I've been there as well. When we forget to live like we've been saved from the dark, demonic forces of evil. Yet we have! Sometimes we'd rather still wallow in the muddy, stink-infected waters rather than recognize what God has done and is still doing in and through us!

Our baptism is only the beginning. It's our daily intentional study of Scripture and our connection with God through prayer that keeps the spectacular event of baptism alive in our memories and continues to grow our faith.

Decide today to live in the truth, fully cleansed, shining His light, and spreading the news of Jesus' living water!

Time in the Truth

- **Genesis 7**
- **Exodus 14**
- **John 4:7-30**
- **John 13:5-16**
- **2 Corinthians 5:14-21**
- **Galatians 2:20**
- **Titus 3:3-7**

Mirror Moment

What is your favorite sound, and why? How does that sound make you feel? Where can you connect this sound to your faith in Jesus?

Now consider the Living Water we've just read about that has been poured out for you. Take time every day this week to let yourself be amazed by this fact: You're guaranteed eternal life with Jesus because of His sacrifice! Live daily in that amazing truth! You are cleansed, sanctified, and justified because of Him!

Communion with my Creator

Dear Provider of Living, Healing Water,

How easily the world, and the noises of it, distract us from the sound of Your voice. It is so easy to miss the echo of the Holy Spirit reminding us of the Power in us because of the precious blood of Your only Son, Jesus. This sacrifice itself brings me to my knees, dear Lord, and the truth of what happened on Calvary's hill makes me stand and raise my hands to praise only You! When I next hear the sound of the river water rushing over the rocks, or stand awed at a waterfall, or simply step into the shower with the water coming from the faucet, I am reminded that I've been cleansed, no longer the old self, but made new and ready to proclaim You wherever I go.

In Jesus' name! Amen

Song Suggestions

Song Title	Artist
Holy Water	We the Kingdom
Dancing on the Waves	We the Kingdom

Theme

Baptism, Living in the Power of Salvation

Discussion Questions following *Rivers, Brooks, and Waterfalls*

1. What are some of your favorite sounds? And why?!

2. Think of each story from Scripture mentioned in the body of the devotional and discuss the power and purpose of water in each one. The stories come from the following Scriptures:

   Genesis 7
   Exodus 14
   John 4:7-30
   John 13:5-16

3. Discuss the posture of one's heart when considering baptism. Discuss if you think one needs to be all cleaned up and have everything figured out in their life to be baptized. Then recognize that baptism is an outward sign of a person who has made a commitment to surrender and live for Him. We don't come to Him clean. He does the cleansing from that moment on.

4. Water baptism is a powerful symbol of new life! Take time to share some of your group's baptism stories? If your baptism wasn't one you have a memory of, consider discussing with a pastor how the outward sign of baptism could be a part of your near future! **And** if you have not yet said yes to the loving salvation of Jesus, please don't be shy about that. Find someone in your group to share with you the freedom and salvation that comes from having a relationship with God and His son, Jesus!

5. **2 Corinthians 5:14-21** is a perfect picture reminding us of our standing with Jesus once we give our lives to Him. Spend time reading each verse and sharing about the power of these words! Then read **Galatians 2:20** and talk about how the reality of this verse should play out in our daily lives once we know Jesus as our Lord and Savior.

6. Be honest with yourselves as you read **Titus 3:3-7**. If you find yourself not believing you are living in the freedom that Jesus provides, how can finding the truth in these words bring you to a place of full surrender and understanding of the power of the cross, knowing it's NOT our works but His sacrifice that makes us righteous?

7. We have been cleansed and made new. We are Holy Spirit vessels. Live like it! Fight for it every day. Listen to one or both of the songs listed as you ponder these incredible truths! Then pray as you close your time together.

17. River Stones

If you're reading this in order, you've just read that water is my favorite sound and my happy place—just watching, listening, and feeling the water trickle, gush, wash, or roar on by! But what I haven't yet shared with you is my great appreciation of river stones. If you've had the great opportunity to observe them, I think you'd agree. They are smooth, often with beautiful markings, and come in different sizes and shapes. The patterns are endless, and their beauty is eye-catching to me. The reason for their beauty is their ability to hold up under the constant flow of water that causes their beauty to appear! Rocks outside the water, or those that haven't encountered massive amounts of water over them, are usually jagged and rough. But that is not the case with river stones.

At the stage of life I am in, I liken myself to a fairly smooth river stone. We are all one in the making, but at different stages. In order to reach "perfect," we must not give up. We must brave what life throws at us. Brace yourself and prepare for a litany of what life can throw at us and how we can respond: *Persevere through illness, endure through loss, learn to process well, patiently march through trying times, wait for outcomes, persist in pain, pursue forgiveness and reconciliation, stand firm against evil, show determination in the face of giants, maintain purpose in the midst of opposition, continue when the game seems over, and carry on when the road seems impossible. The list seems endless. And well, quite overwhelming.

Whew. I'm tired and weary just writing these down, much less stopping to remember some of these trying times in my own life. But these are the things of life we encounter on this planet, as I'm sure many of these resonate with you as well.

How we face and respond to these challenges and meet them head-on will also determine how we finish our race and what our stone will resemble. Who we choose to have as our traveling companion(s) through them is also paramount to how our river stone looks when we "cross the finish line." Only daily communion with our Heavenly Father, through Scripture, prayer, and community with other God-fearing seekers, during the good and the bad times, will make it possible not to end defeated, deflated, and discouraged and become the walking dead. Earthly life has a habit of throwing roadblocks and pitfalls in our way almost every day, but we don't have to fall for them or into them. Preparing beforehand to face them, knowing they are coming, and boldly taking one step at a time, with the guidance of the Holy Spirit giving wisdom to fight through, doesn't take the challenges away, but will certainly provide the fortitude to withstand the heavy waters when they come. We can't escape the pounding water, and if we do somehow, we miss the opportunity to be smooth and beautifully formed. If I might be so bold as to say, "embrace the trial" and "be fearless in the becoming." Be a river stone!

Time in the Truth

- **Job 13:15**
- **Isaiah 54:10**
- **Habakkuk 3:17-19**
- **Daniel 3:8-18**
- **Ephesians 3:11-21**
- **Philippians 4:13**
- **Romans 5:3-5**
- **James 1:2-12**

Mirror Moment

Read through the intense sentence in the body of the devotional beginning with the asterisk*, and take time to pinpoint for yourself the situations that are the most specific to what you are going through or have gone through. Consider how you faced those trials, what you might do differently, and how you can prepare for the ones to come. In faith, read the verses provided and claim them as your own as you face the trials and situations you are currently in. Place your own name in each verse! You're on your way to becoming the most beautiful river stone!

Communion with my Creator

Dearest Lord Jesus,

Life throws blows, but You provide strength. Life pounds, but You sustain. Life says there is no hope, but we know that You are our Hope! Fashion me through my trials as I never stop looking towards You.

In Jesus' name! Amen

Song Suggestions

Song Title	Artist
Do It Again	Elevation Worship
Though You Slay Me	Shane and Shane

Theme

Perseverance, Endurance

Discussion Questions following *River Stones*

1. When you hear the word "rock" or "stone," what comes to mind? Rocks aren't all the same; just ask a geologist! What stands out to you about rocks? What do you know about rocks? Be creative in your answers, even if you aren't a geologist! :)

2. Take time as a group to read again through the devotional, especially the list in the second paragraph. What stage of river rock are you? Read slowly and discuss the questions posed in the Mirror Moment section of this devotional.

3. Job, from Scripture, is likely the frontrunner on knowing what it means to become a river stone... the trials, the betrayal, the shunning, the pain. I find it crazy that this book even exists in Scripture, but it does, meaning God has things to teach us in it! It is filled with such pain, yet encouragement to those who are facing all sorts of trials. **Job 13:15** is Job's declaration that no matter what, his hope is in God. How easy or difficult is this for you when you encounter afflictions?

4. We all know that problems in life are inevitable. How would expecting them instead of being surprised by them change how we live our lives? With this concept in mind, what encouragement can we gain by reading the following verses? **Isaiah 54:10** and **Ephesians 3:11-21**.

5. Hardships can refine us if we have the mindset of learning and growing from and through them. What are your thoughts on this? They can also sometimes result in "a new rhythm under God's direction" that we must accept, which are not always welcomed. What common phrase do you find in these next verses that should be part of accepting those outcomes that are not what we desire? **Habakkuk 3:17-19** and **Daniel 3:8-18**. We have read these verses and discussed the circumstances in previous lessons; however, I believe they are worth revisiting.

6. "I can do all things through Christ who strengthens me." **Philippians 4:13**. How has this simple verse made, or can make, enduring dark nights of the soul possible in your life?

7. **Romans 5:3-5** and **James 1:2-12** seem like an upside-down philosophy in today's society, where we do everything possible not to go through pain or struggles. How can we as believers interpret these verses for ourselves? And if you are struggling to do so, don't hesitate to pray together so you can glean the truth from them and begin to see yourselves as beautiful river stones in the making!

8. Pray each phrase of the Communion prayer, pausing after each one. Ask the Holy Spirit to make these statements real and clear in your life as you face periods of testing; close by listening to one of the songs.

18. Barking Dogs, Chain Saws, No Trespassing, and "More"

Before you wonder if there is never anything out of place or never any conflict on the mountain, I can assure you, this isn't true. The mountain community, and I daresay any community, because they are made up of humans, and we live in a fallen world, isn't perfect by any stretch.

There is the issue of roaming, barking dogs off leashes, and the sides people choose on this and "other" issues. There are noisy chain saws that reverberate and echo that impact solitude. Occasionally we encounter no trespassing signs that dot the walking paths, expressing the attitude of the owners on that stretch of land, and then there is "the More." Yes, more.

I've heard folks speaking of others in less than kind ways, spreading rumors and gossiping, judging the neighbors up or down the hill for one thing or another, making a big deal out of whose trees are whose, and who is responsible for cutting them down if they are dead. Then there is the issue of who should be paying for road repair if it's not on the way to their cabin (many of our roads are privately owned and maintained), the subject of garbage disposal, and on and on it goes. The list doesn't stop there, but I think I will. You get the picture. Concerns that *bring division* exist in every group that involves humans. And our mountain community is no different.

When people are involved, there can be and usually will be a conflict of one sort or another. So, what do we do?

The choice is up to us, on the mountain as well as back at home! We can join in and make more noise, which is sometimes tempting, yet adds to the conflict, resulting in more chaos. We can simply ignore the voices and not say a word. Or better yet, we can speak the truth in love when it's appropriate, be peacemakers, and actually "be love" to those around us through our words and actions. God is love, and we are supposed to imitate Him; therefore, the choice is simple if we are truly what we say we are, Jesus followers. So be Him! And spread shalom (Hebrew for deep and enduring "peace").

Time in the Truth

- **Galatians 5:1**
- **Ephesians 4-5:2**
- **Colossians 3:2,12-17**
- **Hebrews 12:1, 2**
- **1 Peter 1:13-16**
- **Isaiah 53:3-12**

Mirror Moment

Unnecessary conflict sucks. I never use that word, but I have a very adverse attitude to anything unnecessary, especially where hurting others is involved. That being said, very frankly, where can you be a peacemaker in your world today? Where has God placed you that being a peacemaker is what the situation calls for? Not always the most positive position to take, likely risky, but a much-needed insert into the noise of chaos, confusion, and hurting people. Stand up, speak up, and do the right thing in love.

Communion with my Creator

Dear Creator of Peace,

Make me a vessel of Your Presence wherever I go. Give me the strength to remain calm. Restrain my tongue from anything other than the words ordained by You, the discernment to know when to walk away, and always the courage to stand up and speak up for what is true, right, and good, spreading shalom in every corner of our world.

In Jesus' name! Amen

Song Suggestions

Song Title	Artist
Peace, Be Still	The Belonging Co.
He Knows	Jeremy Camp
Peacemaker	Greg Ferguson

Theme
Dealing with Conflict, Peacemaking

Discussion Questions following *Barking Dogs, Chain Saws, No Trespassing, and "More"*

1. Can you think of a person in your life who you consider a peacemaker? If so, what qualities do they possess?

2. Is there a difference between a peacekeeper and a peacemaker? If so, and I believe there is, what is it? Which one provides a more lasting peace?

3. What are some reasons for human conflict? How, as Christians, are we to rise above those emotions and situations? After discussing these questions, how does **Galatians 5:1** speak to both those who bring conflict and chaos versus those who love and obey Jesus?

4. Learning to deal with conflict should begin when we are very young; however, not all methods are effective. What are some positive ways to deal with conflict in your experience? Refer to **Galatians 5:22-26** to guide your answers. Be specific in how these traits can and should help bring peace to our chaotic world of conflict.

5. Read aloud or silently **Ephesians 4 through Ephesians 5:2**. Take note of all the qualities we should possess as Jesus followers in dealing with conflict in regard to others and the old ways we still find ourselves falling into from time to time.

6. After reading **Hebrews 12:1, 2,** discuss what sins can easily entangle us if we don't fix our eyes on Jesus, especially when we deal with difficult or challenging people.

7. In **1 Peter 1:13-16**, we are commanded to prepare our minds for action, to keep sober in spirit, and to set our hope completely on the grace available to us by the revelation of Jesus Christ! How can this command from Peter help us as we strive to be peacemakers?

8. I believe it is humanly impossible to be lasting peacemakers in a world of chaos without the power and peace we are given through Jesus Christ. People today are so easily offended, *including believers.* Remind yourself of the pains Jesus bore for us in the prophecy from **Isaiah 53:1-12**. And how His example and His stripes make it possible for us to continue to be the peacemakers He created us to be! After sitting on this set of verses, is there any doubt we need to show the world, and the world in front of each of us, His peace wherever we are?!

9. Close by listening to one of the song suggestions and praying the Communion Prayer.

Live Shalom!

19. Eagles

A funny thing happened when I chose to write about these birds, which, by the way, are prevalent in our little neck of the woods and the lake below (both Golden and Bald Eagles). I researched online for some general facts about Eagles, but the entire first page was filled with websites for either "Eagles" the band or "Eagles" the football team. So, my lesson for today will be on the clarity and preciseness of our searches.

How often do we fall for someone else's opinion of us or their limited perception of us? I simply typed in the word "eagles," and the web interpreted and chose FOR me two definitions for "eagles" that had nothing to do with what I was searching for.

Who chooses who we are? Who defines for us who and what we are to become? How often do we allow websites, social media, TikTok, YouTube, coworkers, "friends," bosses, or even family members to define who we are, whose we are, and what we are to become? If you have someone, anyone, proclaiming or even insinuating anything other than who God says you are, THEY ARE WRONG! Period.

The age-old question might be, "Who are we, and why are we here?" In my earlier years, I may have allowed too much of others' control and influence to shape or tell me who I am or should be. Looking back, I believe that stems from a lack of self-worth, insecurities, and, for so many, traumatic events. Anything other than God Himself telling us who we are will limit our growth, sway our attentions, deny us the whole truth, and impede God's will and plan for our lives.

After supplying Google with a little more information by being more specific and searching for "eagle, the bird," I found exactly what I was looking for! They are admired the world over as living symbols of power, freedom, and transcendence! With approximately sixty species, they are some of the largest birds and are at the top of the food chain. Their eyesight is amazing, seeing four to five times better than a human ("eagle eye" is a thing, y'all), and they can actually have a wingspan up to ninety-six inches!!!

Now, why am I telling you this, besides it being somewhat interesting? Because whether we are looking for facts about Eagles OR discovering who we are and what we should and can become, we must be intentional in our search. We must ask the right sources and not leave it either to chance or to every Tom, Rick, or Sally to tell us who we are. Choosing wisely so no one else will choose for us is the key! Go to The Source and declare those truths over yourself daily!

Time in the Truth

- **Genesis 2:7**
- **Psalm 139:14-16**
- **John 15:15**
- **Romans 8:15-17**
- **Galatians 2:20**
- **Ephesians 1:5, 6**
- **Ephesians 2:10**
- **Ephesians 3:18, 19**

Mirror Moment

Claim and declare the truths from these verses and remind yourself of them daily!

The lie:	The truth:
I am nothing...	I am made in God's image
I am useless...	I am amazingly and wonderfully knit together
I am hopeless...	I am a fellow heir with Christ
I am a slave to this life...	I am a friend of Jesus
I am stuck with only myself...	I have been crucified with Christ... Christ lives in me
I don't belong...	I am an adopted son/daughter of the King
I am ugly...	I am God's masterpiece

Communion with my Creator

Dear Author of my Life,

I choose to believe what You say about me! I choose to live my life free from the lies of the evil one, whoever he may speak through. I choose to listen to the truth daily and speak life over myself.

In Jesus' name! Amen

Song Suggestion

Song Title	Artist
You Say	Lauren Daigle

Theme

Identity, Choosing Who to Believe

Discussion Questions following *Eagles*

1. Has there been a time in the past or even now when you've allowed others to choose who you are and define you? What power have you given them?

2. When someone creates something, wouldn't you say he/she knows their creation from the inside and out, better than anyone else!? As for God, He created us! Read **Genesis 1:26-28, 31 and 2:7** and discuss how the Creator knows us and what that means to you as His created being!

3. **Psalm 139** is one of my all-time favorite passages of Scripture! Read this Psalm and reflect on the amazing intricacies of human life itself. What are some of your main takeaways from this passage? Do you find it hard to believe the truths in this passage? How should we respond to this Psalm in the way we live?

4. Besides being our Creator, what does **John 15:15-17** say Jesus considers us? How crazy to think that the God of the Universe would call us friends?!!

   And what does He call us to do in this passage?

5. Read **Galatians 2:20**. When feelings of insecurity and a lack of self-worth creep into the perception you have of yourself, how can this passage correct those misconceptions? How does Christ living inside of you change everything?

6. **Romans 8:15-17** takes us deeper into how God feels about us and what His desire is for us! Which part of this passage speaks the loudest to you?

   Consider reading the MSG version to bring more clarity!

   "God's Spirit touches our spirits and *confirms* who we really are."

7. Read these Ephesians passages.

   Ephesians 1:5, 6
   Ephesians 2:10
   Ephesians 3:18, 19

   What does Paul express to us about how precious we are in God's eyes?

8. Which of the lies listed in the Mirror Moments have you believed about yourself, and which of the truths speak to your heart the most? What other lies have you believed, and how is God changing them so you believe what is actually true about you?

9. Close by listening to Lauren Daigle's song and reading the prayer together! Claim these truths for yourself!

20. AirPods and Cell Phones

What is something that is worth spending hours "rescuing" that has gotten stuck between your slatted deck and the metal sheeting a foot below, where there is a point of no return? For me, it's been my young friend's AirPods, my own AirPods, and one of my daughter's cell phones so far. Using broom handles, yardsticks, duct tape, magnets, and once even an electric saw... You name it, and you have a picture of what I've put myself through to restore these items back to whom they belong, after being dusted off, "de-leafed," and "de-pine needled."

Our wonderfully constructed deck that overlooks the beauty of the mountains is also a trap for anything small enough to slide through the slats to the "abyss" a foot below, never to return except by means mentioned in the previous paragraph, along with patience and ingenuity. Call it carelessness or just forgetfulness, I have found that I don't learn my lesson and once again find myself in the "rescue business."

What are we careless with in our lives that can get sucked into a space of either no return or a tough return? This could be any number of things, but we'll focus today on our relationships and how they can slide between the cracks and need rescue and repair. Prepare for a long list of not-so-easy-to-read behaviors: *an off-color remark, a critical spirit, a sarcastic comment, a missed opportunity to support, an assumption or expectation we had that didn't meet our needs or standards, bitterness, resentment, unforgiveness, or just the busyness of life. These can certainly be the stumbling blocks that make us lose our way when it comes to the precious connections we were designed to nurture in our lives.

Our vertical connection with Jesus is the most important relationship we have. Yet it can easily get neglected or pushed to the back burner—and that's never good for navigating life and all its challenges. The same is true of our horizontal relationships. Staying connected with others takes time, commitment, and intention. It requires effort and a willingness to give of ourselves. When we do, and when others invest in us, we all reap the rewards. God blesses us with the fullness of joy that comes through the gift of healthy relationships.

Our deck still has a scar where we cut a piece out to retrieve the dropped phone, but it stands as a reminder to take great care not to drop it again. Maybe we also need a reminder to keep handy so we keep in mind the importance of carefully nourishing and fostering those people in our lives we hold dear.

Time in the Truth

- **Ecclesiastes 4:9-12**
- **Proverbs 4:23**
- **Philippians 4:7**
- **Romans 15:1-7**

- **1 Corinthians 13:4-13**
- **2 Corinthians 13:11-14**

Mirror Moment

What relationship at this moment could use a bit of rescuing, refining, polishing, or at least a good dusting off, and would be worth the time and effort for both of you? We all grieve relationships that aren't what they used to be, but may not know how to make things right or healthy again. *(Some relationships are toxic. These are not the ones I'm referring to here!)*

Now return to the devotional and read carefully the sentence with the asterisk (*), then sit awhile, challenging yourself to pinpoint what part of the slipping away could be your responsibility to mend. Instead of anger, control, blame, or petty feelings, ask God for wisdom on how to move forward to make the first steps in building up instead of continuing to tear down. Even if the relationship can't be restored at this time, or ever, the healing and hard work you do will bring peace to your heart and maybe one day do the same for the other person(s) as well.

There are so many variables and layers to restoring relationships. Find a sober mentor, therapist, or pastor to confide in to help you walk this journey.

Communion with my Creator

To the God who created relationships,

To the God who restored our relationship with Him,

To the God who's been mending broken relationships since the dawn of time,

We come before You with our brokenness and hurt and pain of the relationships we have here on Earth, seeking answers and steps for restoration.

Help us lay down the distractions and lies the enemy so cunningly has put in our way in order to pick up the healthy tools needed to bring healing. Give us boldness to take the first step.

In Jesus' name! Amen

Song Suggestions

Song Title	Artist
Restoration	David Brymer
Forgiveness	Matthew West

Theme
Nurturing and Repairing Relationships

Discussion Questions following *AirPods and Cell Phones*

1. Have you ever lost something that you can still see or know where it is, but it's just out of reach? What lengths did you go to in order to get it back? Or maybe you didn't.

2. What is the reason you often let relationships slip into disrepair? Refer to the sentence in the body of the devotional with the asterisk in the third paragraph for help in answering this question.

3. Brevity of life often brings clarity to what needs to be mended and accomplished. Therefore, pretend for a moment you are very near the end of your life, and you are assessing your regrets when it comes to your relationships. How does this scenario change the way you see those relationships that are tarnished and "just out of reach"?

4. Consider a human relationship that has slipped down beneath the slats and needs to be rescued. What effort would be appropriate to make it healthy again? Stop right now in your group and pray for those you are thinking about, without naming any names. You could also pair up for the next few minutes to do the same.

5. How do the verses in **Ecclesiastes 4:9-12** address the need for human bonds?

6. It is true that not all of our human relationships need to be revived, due to the toxic nature of the connection, or the other person(s). How does **Proverbs 4:23** speak to this truth? And how does **Philippians 4:7** help remind us to guard our hearts when we've done all we can to try and mend an unmendable relationship?

7. When reading **Romans 15:1-7**, ask God for a healthy dose of conviction and what it means to put others' needs before our own. IF it is pride, anger, bitterness, or unforgiveness that is driving the wedge in your relationship, what should your next step be?

8. How do the following phrases play a role in the divisiveness of friendships? "It's his/her turn to call me," "I can't believe he/she said that about me," "I can't believe he/she didn't invite me to this or that," "I'm just too busy," etc. Do you recognize the common denominator here... self... the "I's" have it! Remind yourself of the true meaning of love in **1 Corinthians 13:4-13** and that God calls us to love like He does.

9. Finally, as you read **2 Corinthians 13:11-14**, discuss the list of things Paul encourages the church at Corinth to do. The church in Corinth had many interpersonal struggles. We see them in 1 and 2 Corinthians. These verses are the final words he had with them! What can and should we learn from God's words through Paul?

10. Close with the Communion Prayer and listen to one of the suggested songs, being reminded that Jesus was OUR restoration, so we should be willing to do the same for others.

21. My View is Better than Yours
Part 1

I have to admit, we bought our cabin for the view! The inside was roomy and nice enough, but it needed quite a makeover. We were captivated by the incredible beauty of the mountains from the deck. It never ceases to provide the perfect view! I have mentioned our view several times, but I'd like to share a different perspective with you today.

When we walk the area, we check out the other cabins' views from their decks if they have one, and are pretty sure we scored high on the list of cabins with the best views! Others have actually said they are jealous of our view or would love to have the view we do. We usually tell them they are welcome to come up and enjoy it! But it is ours ;). Not to gloat too much... A takeaway from this is the danger of pride, as well as the dangerous activity of comparison. Today we'll be tackling the latter.

Stay tuned for Part 2 and the unbecoming puffing up of pride.

As for comparison, this practice or activity never ends well. And when it gets a foothold, it can consume us. Comparison should not even be in our vocabulary. It certainly shouldn't be practiced on more than anything but a view from a cabin. "What you have, I want," or "What you can afford, I can't," or "What you are looking forward to, I never can!" are dangerous mental games we sadly find ourselves playing long after we leave middle school. This way of thinking has all the key ingredients to make us miserable and drive wedges between us and others.

If and when you can get close enough to examine how you've compared, things usually aren't as rosy as they look anyway. Besides my thoughts on the subject, comparison has never been God's plan. He has a plan for each of us. Each plan looks different. Each plan has a purpose in His grand blueprint for those He loves and sacri-

← ONE OF LITERALLY 100'S OF PHOTOS WE'VE TAKEN FROM OUR DECK. DON'T FORGET TO USE MY QR CODE TO SEE THE COLOR PHOTOS FOR EACH LESSON!

ficed for, which is all of us. It's not looking at anyone else's life. It's about making the very best of ours and following hard after the opportunities He has designed for each one of us.

Getting back to my metaphor... As I wander down the hill from our cabin, I spot many cabins nestled cool inside the tall piney woods and forest away from the winds, those winds that often make it hard for us to sit and enjoy being outside just up the hill. There are also those cabins even farther below, built near the lower streams, where you can sit outside and listen to the water gurgling by. These views and sounds are glorious in themselves. I hope you understand my point. Just like every cabin has its blessings, so do we.

Take inventory and find your blessings. The joy comes from finding the beauty everywhere. Not of your neighbors' views, but of yours!

Time in the Truth

- Matthew 7:12
- Romans 12:2-8
- 1 Corinthians 13:4
- 2 Corinthians 10:12, 17-18
- Galatians 6:4, 5
- 1 Timothy 6:6-8
- James 1:17
- James 3:13-18 (MSG)

Mirror Moment

Looking in the mirror to reflect on the topic of comparison can be painful. Are we really that petty? It's a sad "normal" part of young teens, but when carried into our adult lives, it is a poison that affects our relationships and our own well-being. Where have you compared? Where are you comparing even now? Has any comparison been helpful in your life? What causes you to compare? Take time to answer these questions personally and then find reasons to be grateful for what you have. **A spirit of gratitude is the opposite of a spirit of comparison, and it's where God wants our minds and hearts to live.**

Communion with my Creator

Dear Giver of all good gifts,

You have gifted me and blessed me with _____. You have provided for me by _____. When my eyes wander and I begin to either think more of myself or what I have than I should, or lean toward feeling less blessed or gifted, bring me back to the place of realizing that You alone are all I need. I release those insecure feelings that make me believe I need to be like others or have what others have. Replace those feelings with Your truth that "I am enough," "You are enough for me," "I am made unique and beautiful," "You love me," and "I love me, too!"

In Jesus' name! Amen

Song Suggestions

Song Title	Artist
Priceless	For King and Country
Comparison Kills	Jonathan McReynolds

Theme
Deadly Practice of Comparison, Being Grateful

Discussion Questions following *My View is Better than Yours, Part 1*

1. Is there any area of your life where you find yourself comparing yourself to others? Or have in the past? What kinds of emotions do these memories bring up?

2. What is the best way to counter the trap of comparison?

3. Read **Matthew 7:12**. The Golden Rule is one of those concepts thought of as important even to those who don't believe in God. Why is that? And what happens when we get caught up in the negativity of comparison that makes living by the Golden Rule impossible?

4. After reading **Romans 12:2-8** consider these questions:

   a. What does "transformed by the renewing of our minds" look like?

   b. How does the sin of comparison keep us from discovering and using our own gifts?

5. Read **1 Corinthians 13:4**. How is comparing unloving?

6. Read **2 Corinthians 10: 12, 17-18**. The MSG version mentions comparing, grading, and competing as "missing the point." How do we undermine the work of God in our lives when we find ourselves using these "unhealthy tools" in our lives?

7. **Galatians 6:4, 5 (MSG)** are powerful verses for counteracting comparison living! Reading further into this chapter reveals the two outcomes depending on how we live our lives. Discuss the differences.

8. What quality mentioned in **1 Timothy 6:6-8** dispels the destructive nature of comparison? What are the lasting benefits of this quality?

9. How does remembering the truth found in **James 1:17** correct our perspective? How is the deception of comparison dishonoring to God?

10. Read **James 3:13-18**. Finally, how does growing in wisdom feed contentment and gratitude?

11. Spend some time being grateful :). Fill in the blanks in the Communion Prayer and listen to the song suggestions as you close your gathering today.

22. My View is Better than Yours Part 2

"First pride, then the crash—the bigger the ego, the harder the fall."
—Proverbs 16:18 (MSG)

I have found that people with big egos and lots of pride are always out to prove themselves. On the outside, they first appear in control, usually as leaders who appear to know what they are doing, in order to get things done. Yet, underneath the very thin, shiny facade is the truth. The truth is that they are usually **out** of control, spinning in circles, making everyone think things are grand and amazing, when instead they are miserable and falling apart. They use intimidation and whatever means to make everything about themselves. Most prideful individuals come across as bullies and brats, except to other bullies and brats; and then they wallow in the mire together, making everyone else wretchedly uncomfortable! Somewhere along the road, they learned that the way to being accepted and worthy is to make everyone else feel small and insignificant. This certainly doesn't justify their actions, but it may give us insight into understanding why they act the way they do.

The newest fashion, the latest model, the biggest whatever. Look at me, look at what I can do, look at me! Ok, I'll stop now, but I'm almost certain everyone reading this can think of at least one person, or maybe multiple people, who fit this category and have made, or are making, your life miserable. I'm painting a picture for you of how ugly a person with pride can look, or can grow into, if untamed and unharnessed. And a willful child whose willfulness isn't broken can easily find themselves in this place as they grow up.

The person with the biggest deck, in this case me, could slip into that trap. I could rub into everyone's faces how good we have it, how our place is the end-all, yet at any minute a big bad wind could blow a tree into our deck, and we'd be ruined, or a fire could come along and burn it all down.

It's easy to look at others and see their prideful ways. But let's look a little closer to "home." I hope and pray under no circumstances the ugly picture I just painted in the previous paragraphs is me, or ever will be. But we must all be honest with ourselves and ask if we ever have those thoughts or temptations to place ourselves above others. If we have any tendency towards pride, we should take a long look in the mirror and root it out. Be kind. No measurement is necessary.

Don't be that person; AND, be on guard against that kind of person in your life, not falling into the trap of allowing them to win at their game of making you feel less than.

Time in the Truth

- **Proverbs 11:2, 3**
- **Proverbs 25:14-16**
- **Romans 12:2, 3 (4-21)**
- **1 Corinthians 13:4**
- **Philippians 2:3-18**
- **James 4:6 (4:1-17)**
- **Psalm 139:23, 24**

Mirror Moment

The flip side of pride is where we will begin our reflection today. The counter to pride is humility. Begin with humility, and the pride piece will not be able to grow. Begin by seeing others as more important than ourselves, and we'll never use them as stepping stones to our achievements. Begin by being compassionate, and we won't ever treat anyone as disposable. Begin to live in the joy, purpose, and love found in Jesus, and we won't have to hurt others to feel better about ourselves. Begin with the best definition of love **(1 Corinthians 13:4-7)**, and there'll be no room for hate.

Communion with my Creator

Dear Forgiving Father,

I come to You with a repentant heart. There are situations where I've placed myself above others, acted out of pride, and obviously hurt people along the way. I have thought too much of myself and wanted to get ahead, and in the process, made others feel less than. I admit the pain I've caused and am sorry for hurting others and putting myself in the place only You should and deserve to be. Please correct MY view of myself. "Create in me a pure and clean heart, O God, and renew a steadfast spirit within me." Help me take off the robe of pride and replace it with one of humility and obedience to You.

For those who have treated me unjustly and made me feel unworthy and less than, remind me of the worth I have in You and of the gifts and love You so freely shower on me.

In Jesus' name! Amen

Song Suggestions

Song Title	Artist
Nothing Else	Cody Carnes
Empty Me	Chris Sligh
Humble King	Brenton Brown

Theme

Deadly Practice of Pride

Discussion Questions following *My View is Better than Yours, Part 2*

1. Consider the Proverb mentioned at the beginning of this devotional. Can you think of someone to whom this has happened, either personally or in public life?

2. Read the following: **Proverbs 11:2, 3; 25:14-16**. Then answer questions 3 and 4.

3. Define the word "pride" in your own words, using synonyms and short phrases. Continue the conversation with what usually becomes of relationships when a person like this is encountered. Consider the metaphor in **Proverbs 25:14** when answering.

4. Consider the opposite, or antonyms, of pride. Do the same by discussing what usually follows in a relationship if a person has these qualities. In the Proverbs you just read, use some of the opposite qualities of pride to give you a head start :).

5. Let's take a look in the mirror, since we may not always recognize when pride creeps into our own lives. Take time to read and discuss the Mirror Moment and **Romans 12:2, 3** to add more to your discussion. You can also expand your reading to include the remainder of **Romans 12** to enrich your study together, as it speaks to *honoring everyone's differing gifts and the value God places on putting others before ourselves.*

6. Paul again speaks of the importance of humility to the believers in Philippi, in **Philippians 2:3-18**. However, this time, he paints the picture of how Jesus is our example of a life lived free from pride. Read it with fresh eyes, embracing the powerful words expressing how living a life of humility is much greater than a life of pride could ever be.

7. Finally, or almost finally, what is the blessing God gives to those who are humble in **James 4:6**? For further study, read all of **James 4**.

8. Now, finally, after all this discussion on pride, if you've found even the slightest hint of this in your own life (and likely we all have at one time or another), begin with the Communion With the Creator prayer and end by reading aloud **Psalm 139:23, 24** inserting YOUR own name in place of the word "me" each time; then listen to any one of the three song suggestions listed.

23. Painful Arrows

Being on "mountain time" means many things to many folks. It may mean turning off the brain from the rigorous life we live daily back home and reading a good book. It can mean having time to take a walk and not be disturbed. Sometimes it means sitting for hours staring at the beauty and stillness of nature. It also means taking a nap in the middle of the day and getting much-needed rest. I have experienced a bit of all of these since we became cabin owners; however, one thing is for certain: "mountain time" always means having enough time to stop and think.

Thinking on the "not-so-happy" memories we've endured at the hands of others is where we will land today. The ache inflicted on our hearts, minds, souls, and even bodies when others have used us as target practice for their quiver of arrows. This can be harsh and ugly to think about, but it's a reality in all of our lives. If left unaddressed, they can cause us more pain, angst, anxiety, depression... open wounds that just won't heal. And who needs or deserves that?

Flushing out and dealing with these memories can be and usually is good once we do it. But it certainly isn't easy. I'd like to interject that seeing a trained therapist is one of the best ways to deal with this heartache, but "the mountain" and a good "mountain friend" can be a good starting point, whether you are in the mountains or not.

I've personally done this on my own. Forcing myself to spend time alone praying, journaling, crying, letting go, and praying some more. All until the issues I've needed to address don't have the same power over me that they did before I took the time to stop, surrender, be real with myself and my emotions, and yes, even recognize my part in the pain.

I've also been on the listening end of others' pain when on the mountain, on more than one or two occasions. You see, mountain time lends itself to such a process if we let it. You know, the conversation starts light and airy, discussing the clouds over the peaks or the birds in the trees, and turns deep and heavy because there is trust, and there is time. Trusting that our conversations will remain confidential, and time, lots of it. Time necessary to speak, to be silent, to offer comfort and suggestions of how to move forward, and to be real.

Arrows and darts targeted at our hearts are not only painful and leave scars, but can also become paralyzing. Don't settle for a band-aid on a gaping hole in your heart. Get some wound care started. Pick through your thoughts, and pray hard, asking Jesus to reveal what you need to know about the pain. Find a trusted "mountain friend," whether you are ever in the mountains or not. And also, consider finding a therapist.

Time in the Truth

- **Psalm 34:18**
- **Psalm 147:3**
- **Isaiah 61:1-7**
- **2 Corinthians 4:8, 9**
- **Psalm 27:2-3, 10**

Mirror Moment

Write your own prayer today that will begin to address the pain you've endured from others. It's okay to be raw, real, and honest. It's the only way God has the opportunity to start the process of removing the arrow, cleaning out the wound, and allowing healing to take place.

Use my prayer on the next page if needed to guide you in writing your own.

Communion with my Creator

Dear Healer of my Wounded Soul,

I have been hurt. Hurt by someone I've loved. Hurt by someone I thought loved me. Hurt by someone I've worked for. Hurt by my friend. It makes me sad. Even more, it makes me angry. I feel used and abused. Their pride, ego, anger, and power have made me feel less than and marginalized. By myself, I can't begin to heal or even know where to start the healing process. By myself, I can't make the scars from this pain lessen. I can make no sense of it. Asking others to help me only temporarily eases the sadness. I need You. I need You to help me process the crippling ache that comes from the trespass of others. This offense is personal, and I can't deny it. I know I can lay it down, and You can take the wound and tend to it tenderly. Teach me through this. Make me wiser and stronger. Let this be a lesson, always a lesson, so I can grow. Train me to be bold enough to stand against the mean cruelty of others by taking a stand for what's right, not picking sides. Help me know where to expend my energy, where it will be received, and where it will not be wasted. Give me wisdom to know when to place those who won't change or aren't interested in reconciliation into a separate category in my mind and heart that won't deplete me or my joy for today.

Thank You for Your listening ear and for Your concern for Your children.

I give You ALL the praise and the glory, O Lord God!

In Jesus' name! Amen

*This prayer was written as I wrestled alone in my thoughts on the mountain over pain I've felt from others.

Song Suggestion

Song Title	Artist
I Am No Victim	Kristene DiMarco

Theme

Healing for the Victim

Discussion Questions following *Painful Arrows*

Today's group discussion may be challenging since it is so personal. However, attempt to consider the folks in your group your "mountain friends." And go only as far as you feel safe with opening up. But remember, "You can't heal what you don't reveal."

1. Have you ever done or competed in archery? If so, did you enjoy it, and were you good at it?

2. After reading the devotional together, individually read the Communion with the Creator prayer to yourselves and pinpoint the archer or archers who have thrown deadly arrows your way. After doing so, take a scrap piece of paper and write the initials of the person(s) responsible for your hurt and tuck it away for a little later. For the remainder of this study on Painful Arrows, consider this person(s) as you work through the pain.

3. What are some of the key points that stood out to you, either in the body of the devotional or the prayer you just read?

4. Read **Psalm 34:18** and talk about what His nearness means to those who are hurting and what it means to be delivered. Then read **Psalm 147:3**. God is the One who heals! And nothing is too hard for Him! What does healing and bandaging our hearts look like for you? Read further into **Psalm 34** to further enlighten your discussion.

5. Read **Isaiah 61:1-7**. In this passage, it tells us God is commissioned to help the brokenhearted, and instead of shame and humiliation, they will receive a double portion and experience LASTING joy! Do you believe this? What does the process look like in going from shame and humiliation to having lasting joy? Again, if time allows, read the remainder of **Isaiah 61** to deepen your understanding.

6. Discuss some of the possible variables in the process you just discussed and how long this journey could take. Is the process always linear? If you haven't already discussed emotions, how do our emotions play a big role in both the pain and the healing? How does Satan try to use our emotions against us on the road to healing?

7. Spend a period of time in your group writing your own prayer, using mine as a jumping-off place. Make it more personal considering the arrows that have wounded you.

8. Be encouraged and reminded of God's faithfulness to always be with us by reading the following verses: **Psalm 27:2-3, 10** and **2 Corinthians 4:8, 9**.

9. As you close, listen to the suggested song. While doing so, pray the prayer you wrote, and if you feel you can, tear up the scrap of paper you wrote on earlier, signifying that person(s) has no more power over you!

24. Lanie the Labradoodle

Lanie is our adorable labradoodle! She lives by the rules in the city... She stays inside or in the fenced backyard, is on a leash when we walk, or is safely in the car when she rides with us. She sleeps in her closed kennel at night and roams about the confines of the house during the day.

But then, one awesome day, she experienced the cabin in midwinter, when there are hardly any residents on the mountain. FRRREEEEEDDDDDOMMMMMMM!

This may sound extreme, but to see her run free back and forth through the newfallen snow all over our property, and our neighbors' too, is to watch the purest sense of NO leash, NO harness, NO restrictions, NO rules—ONLY complete and utter freedom!

Did you know this is how God wants us to live?! He's the God of grace and mercy, of faithfulness and goodness, of righteousness and truth, and of unconditional love for those who are called by His name!

But we find ourselves tethered to the harnesses and leashes and kennels, never truly understanding the freedom we can and should live by when we accept the forgiveness, grace, and hope of Jesus Christ. For some, this may come easily, but for others of you, it may sound like an impossibility because of how life and others have treated and spoken to you—but it isn't out of your reach. This freedom Jesus offers is available to everyone for the asking. Don't miss out; don't spend your days leashed up!

Now, Lanie knows who feeds her, who loves her, and who provides for her. So, she doesn't go far, and she always—okay, mostly—comes when we call the first time. This freedom isn't without boundaries, but it is invigorating, life-giving, and permission-giving to explore new and wonderful adventures. Try listening to the voice of God's invitation to be free from the things that burden you by surrendering and leaving them at the cross. And choose to live there!

← LANIE ENJOYS THE BEAUTIFUL SCENERY AS MUCH AS WE DO!

If I'm oversimplifying how we should respond to God's gift of freedom, that is not my intention. I know it isn't always as simple as my story of Lanie. Seek counsel, seek wisdom, and listen closely to the loving voice of Jesus as He calls you to the place where He always wanted you to reside. And there you'll find that *the truth of God* (not the legalism of rules) and *the grace of God* (not the license to do anything you please) are where the **truest** and **purest** place of FREEDOM resides.

Now breathe.

Time in the Truth

- **John 3:16**
- **Hebrews 10:1-25**
- **John 8:31-36**
- **2 Corinthians 3:12-18**
- **Galatians 5:1, 13**

Mirror Moment

Where do you feel stuck, or "on a leash"? What thoughts do you speak to yourself or have been spoken over you that cause you to be bound, haunted, and caged? Speak them aloud, take them to the Good Father, and, like I've mentioned several times before, a well-trained therapist. Begin the path to freedom and liberation from any lies and deception. He wants you to be set free and live! It may be a long journey, but it's worth it.

Communion with my Creator

Dear Freedom Giver,

Lies and deception, pain and hurt have kept me from living free. There are the lies others have told me, and I've believed them and tell them to myself now. There are deceptive manipulations that were imposed upon me, and I've accepted them as part of who I am. But I so desperately desire the freedom that comes from recognizing lies from truth. Knowing the real truth, accepting the truth, and believing the truth is meant for me. I'm ready to do the work to reach the place of freedom. Give me boldness to stand against the falsehoods and recognize my worth, my beauty, and my place in this world.

In Jesus' name! Amen

Song Suggestions

Song Title	Artist
I Speak Jesus	Charity Gayle
Egypt	Cory Asbury
My Chains are Gone/Amazing Grace	Chris Tomlin

Theme

Deliverance, Freedom

Discussion Questions following *Lanie the Labradoodle*

1. Do you have a dog? If so, can he/she be off-leash? If not, have they ever gotten out? What were the consequences?

2. **John 3:16,17** is probably the most recited and known verse in Scripture. Today, read it in a variety of translations and discuss the impact of these few lines. Examine who Jesus is talking to and why this conversation and what Jesus says here are so powerful!

3. Pore over **Hebrews 10:1-25**. These verses address the stark differences between the Old Covenant and the New Covenant. Compare the difference once Jesus' life was given in place of ours, AND the countless sacrifices needed prior to Jesus' death, in order to be clean and whole. How do these comparisons relate to the bondage we sometimes live in today?

4. Being early listeners of Jesus' words must have been confusing to the Jewish people. Read **John 8:31-36** with this in mind. Also, take note of the word "truth," and how truth and grace go hand in hand. They are not opposites. They complement one another! How is this concept still hard for us today? Hint: Truth without grace is just the law/slavery. Grace without truth is license to do as one pleases. What do we gain when we embrace and live with both grace and truth?

5. Read **2 Corinthians 3:12-18 (MSG)**. This passage expresses the freedom that comes from a relationship with Jesus, versus us living in bondage. What life experiences have caused you to remain fettered, not fully receiving the freedom we've been discussing? Don't stop here. Read the powerful verses in question 6!

6. Lastly, read **Galatians 5:1 and 13-15** (love these in MSG, too). If you still have questions about God wanting you to live in freedom, relish the truth put forth in these verses.

7. Pray over and consider laying gentle hands on those who still live shackled by chains. Ask the Holy Spirit to remove those restraints and begin to make the verses about freedom you read today a reality!! Close by choosing one of the powerful song suggestions and let the words sing over you!

25. Night Sky Part 1: Stars

For this city girl, truly seeing the night sky without the distraction of lights from homes, buildings, and signs came with an absolute feeling of awe. I'm not sure I can describe it with words. The millions of stars, and I don't think I'm exaggerating, that can be seen on a clear night from the mountain call for me to pause, raise my hands to Heaven, and give awesome praise to the Creator of it all.

Scripture says He calls each star by name! He also told Abram his descendants would outnumber the stars! In my opinion, until you see them from an unhindered surrounding, you don't get the full picture or understanding of these mentions in the Bible, or just how awesome God's immense creation is.

Once we are old enough to know what a star truly is, how far it is from us, and how we are seeing the light from a star many years later, that about does it for me. I mean, it wraps up the feeling of awe and makes it... well, indescribable.

I really want you to continue this devotional yourself. With words, phrases, or sentences about how awesome God is! Where have you seen Him show up, like a sky full of stars for you? Or witnessed His goodness years after you begged Him in prayer to answer, but now are finally witnessing the silver lining? The stars understand. Their light doesn't show up for us to see for a very long time, yet they keep shining as long as possible. They shine as brightly as they can until they burn up, knowing the light they created is for years later when our eyes behold it. Abraham learned this lesson as well. It wasn't until years after being told his descendants would outnumber the stars that he would see the beginning of his lineage.

Stars. They are reminders of how Big and Almighty and Powerful our God is. Beyond Big. Worship Him today with abandon, like the stars shining in a night sky! And grasp, at least slightly, how, if *you* choose to shine your light, it will benefit those long after you! Light up your own world... Be a Star!

Time in the Truth

- **Genesis 15:5, 6**
- **Psalm 147:3-5**

- **Matthew 5:13-16**

Mirror Moment

Your mirror moment was worked into the devotional itself today. Answer the questions posed, and remind yourself you are worthy of shining brightly!!

Communion with my Creator

Dear Star Namer,

If You created the stars and took the time to name each one, how much more do You care for me, the one You said shares Your imprint and was made in Your image?

You've named me Your heir, You've named me Your adopted child, and You've named me unique, bold, strong, redeemed, upheld, masterfully crafted, a friend of the King, and beloved!

In return, I am in awe of You. I call You Faithful. I call You my best Friend, I call You Abba, Daddy. I call You Master, my Banner, my Peace, my Healer, and my Provider.

(Don't stop with my list. Make it as long as you can. Page after page of names that demand our attention and are rightfully His!)

I bring my honor and praise to You. My awe and wonder as well!

In Jesus' name! Amen

Song Suggestion

Song Title	Artist
Indescribable	Chris Tomlin

Theme

The Awe of God, Being a Light, Perseverance

(Chapter 25 and 26 can be combined. Questions following 26 apply to both chapters.)

26. Night Sky Part 2: Shooting Stars!

As long as we are on the topic of stars, I can't forget to mention the shooting stars we see regularly! In a world of instant replays, or "watch again" movies, shows, and videos on YouTube, "shooting stars" don't shout or make any noise, and they certainly don't repeat. They are one and done. They just happen, and you had better be watching. I may see one, and my husband doesn't, or vice versa. We can only try to describe it to the other and keep scanning the sky for another, in hopes we'll spot several more before our early bedtime these days.

This is a very enjoyable evening activity in the mountains, but relates easily to our lives. Are we watching expectantly for God to show us something new each day? Or do we find ourselves so bogged down by the daily grind, the weight of whatever is troubling us, or the distractions of all kinds that we can't see the beauty right in front of us, as well as the chances to brighten someone's day and be their shooting star moment for the day? The opportunity of seeing a shooting star demands our attention and patience, and if we miss it, we will never be able to see that one again and will have to wait for another. The opportunities God places in our lives daily also demand our attention and patience, knowing He is ready and willing to show us if we remain alert and expectant. With the understanding and stark reality that the time and place we are in right now will never repeat itself ever again, just like a shooting star, we must make the most of every golden chance presented!

Scan the horizon, be watchful for the beauty and the possibility to be the beauty for someone else, all the while thanking God for His chances to make the most out of life, every minute. Seize the day!

Time in the Truth

- Psalm 90:12
- Ephesians 5:15-17
- Colossians 4:5, 6
- 1 John 2:17

Mirror Moment

When you look in the mirror, recognize and proclaim you are fearfully and wonderfully crafted and made with a purpose for today! When you walk out of your door to go about your day, keep your focus on what God can show you—someTHING you haven't noticed before, or someONE. Make the most of both, actively participating in the miracle of that moment!

Communion with my Creator

Dear Awe-Inspiring Almighty,

There are definitely seasons where I don't seize the days I live in. For whatever reasons I have, I now confess that they are really only excuses for not doing Your will for me today. I aim to change that now and every day after. I'll come back tonight, or tomorrow, and finish this prayer! I will be thanking You for the opportunity You showed me, and what I did when I recognized it! I'm ready for "a shooting star," Lord.

In Jesus' name! Amen

(And don't forget to come back and finish this prayer!)

Song Suggestion

Song Title	Artist
Stars in the Sky	Kari Jobe

Theme

Expectancy

Discussion Questions following *Night Sky*
Part 1

1. What is one of your favorite names or attributes of God?

2. What is one of the number one things that distracts or hinders your ability to experience God?

3. Where have you seen God show up when you've least expected?

4. After reading **Genesis 15:5, 6** consider how long Abram had to wait for this promise to come true. What did Sarah and Abram do in the meantime, trying to speed God's promise along and "help" it come to pass? How does knowing this translate to our own lives?

5. After reading **Psalm 147:3-5**, what do you think is the psalmist's reason for telling us God names each of the stars? What qualities of God come to mind knowing this fact?

6. In **Matthew 5:13-16** we are asked to be the salt of the earth and to shine our light. Consider how being salt, as well as shining God's light, coupled with trusting God's timing, His Sovereign plan, can be the perfect combination with the perfect outcome? Why is this sometimes hard for us?

Part 2

1. **Psalm 90:12** teaches us to number our days that we may present to Him a heart of wisdom. Another reminder of this is in Paul's letter to the Ephesians when he reminds them in **Ephesians 5:15-17** to make the most of their time. Time along with wisdom are both key elements in these passages. What can and should we learn about time and wisdom that will provide the truth we need to live our lives to the fullest?

2. Being expectant to see God work in our everyday lives should become our norm. What does living with a God-expectant mindset provide for us and others, and how can we choose this daily?

3. Choose one or both of the song suggestions to listen to. Personalize your prayer to the awe-inspiring Star Namer!

27. Clouds Part 1: Imagination and Innovation

One definition for the word "imagination" is "forming a mental image of something and having creative ability."

I've always enjoyed cloud watching. It may sound childish, and that was when I began to watch clouds, but as an adult I still enjoy it! Whether I'm sitting on the deck in the mountains or simply sitting back at home looking up, I 'cloud watch', finding dragons, puppy dogs, and trains in the sphere above before they quickly morph into something completely different.

I assumed everyone had the "ability" to imagine until someone told me they'd never been given the chance. Their life had been one filled with nothing but survival mode. The ability to relax, let alone dream and imagine, had never been nurtured or even permitted in her home growing up.

This saddened me, as I believe God created us to be imaginative, creative, and filled with dreams for our lives. Being able to let our minds flow from what we see, and feel, and wander for a bit, is all part of processing, discovering, and growing, which leads to bigger dreams and visions that He purposely created for us!

I found a few synonyms for the word "imagination" that I'd like to share with you: resourcefulness, originality, and invention! Wow! Imagination has value way beyond staring at the clouds. But nurturing our ability to form mental images and stopping to imagine what we could become and what life might look like in the future can definitely lead to a new reality! One that was meant for you, if you take the time to dream!

I don't watch the clouds every day or spend my days daydreaming, but I do encourage allowing imagination of what could be and dream big... beyond the borders of what is! Because, my friends, that is just what God is in the business of doing!

← A SKY VIEW NEVER CEASES TO AMAZE ME,
  EVER CHANGING AND FILLED WITH AWE!

Time in the Truth

- **Psalm 37:4-7**
- **Proverbs 3:5-13**
- **Jeremiah 29:4-14**

- **Mark 9:23, 24**
- **John 14:12**
- **Ephesians 2:4-10**

Mirror Moment

Throughout Scripture, men and women had visions and dreams: Moses, Abraham, Joseph, Hannah, Jeremiah, David, Joseph (Jesus' earthly father), and the Wise Men, to name a few. They saw beyond what was and believed and trusted in what could and would become real!

If we believe in Jesus, then we believe in a spiritual realm bigger, greater, and more real than what we see with our human eyes. We might start with clouds and what we see. Yet, when we allow ourselves to dream big and **ask God** for what He has planned for us, we can and will be blown away and find God's plans are beyond our wildest dreams or imaginations. Don't limit Him and His dreams for you. The dreams of those in Scripture and the prophecies we read about were only realized when those given them believed and trusted the process. So today, **believe** in a big dream.

Communion with my Creator

Dear Dream Spinner,

I trust You to continue to work in my life as long as I have breath in my lungs. I'm courageously asking You, Jesus, to show up big! I believe You did it in the days of old and are the same today as You were then. Remove any unbelief, and replace it with a bold faith, ready for whatever You desire.

In Jesus' name! Amen

Song Suggestion

Song Title	Artist
Dream For You	Casting Crowns

Theme
Innovation, Dreams

Discussion Questions following *Clouds Part 1*

1. What is your definition of "creative," and do you consider yourself an imaginative person?

2. What is your definition of "imagine?" Do you find yourself envisioning and visualizing? Why or why not? Listen to Casting Crowns' "Dream for You" :).

3. Look at the list of "dreamers" and visionaries in the Mirror Moments. Choose one or more of these Biblical characters and consider the following:

   a) How realistic were their visions at the time they had them?

   b) Who believed in them?

   c) What did the "dreamers" do with their vision? How did their lives turn out?

4. Read **Psalm 37:4-7**. Discuss the phrase "desires of your heart" in context with the rest of this passage. What must be "in sync" in order for our dreams to come to pass?

5. How does the passage in **Proverbs 3:5-13** continue with this same message, and what more can we glean from it when it comes to our dreams?

6. Read **Jeremiah 29:4-14**. What a power-packed passage!!! God's people felt abandoned, their dreams dashed, having been exiled in Babylon. Read all that God shared with them and asked them to do. What blessings did He give them so they didn't give up? What can we learn from these verses on how to live our lives? (Consider reading this passage in the MSG version as well.)

7. What truth is made clear by Jesus in **Mark 9:23, 24**, and what can we learn from the response of the boy's father? How does our disbelief about the spiritual world keep us from receiving God's miracles and plans for us?

8. If you've ever doubted what God can do in your life, the message in **Philippians 4:13** counteracts that lie. How does the truth spoken here bring courage to your dreams and visions? (No matter your age, stage, or station in life.)

9. As Jesus was speaking to his apostles, nearing the end of his earthly life, He said to them, "... the one who believes in Me, the works that I do, he will do also; and greater works than these he will do..." It's hard to believe, but it's right there in red print, Jesus' own words. Everything is possible with Jesus! Allow God to use you mightily as you boldly imagine what He has for you to do!

10. Would anyone care to share a dream or vision they have and are waiting for God to bring it to pass? And close with prayer.

28. Clouds Part 2: Casting Shadows

Clouds cast shadows, different ones every day. They allow sunlight to shine around them, spreading brilliant colors below. We may prefer cloudless days, but clouds bring dimension to the land. If you've ever watched the sun rising or setting, it's the clouds in perfect spaces that make for the magnificent rays to shoot up from the horizon. As you can imagine, this is another reason I love clouds! The awe-inspiring view we have the privilege of looking at from our deck changes every day. Oh, it's the same mountain and the same trees. It's the same contour of the land, yet it looks different every day, changing multiple times a day, depending on the hour, the placement of the sun, and the clouds!

Let's consider for a moment that clouds are the "hard" of life. And the landscape is our life we face daily. Life, if we are honest, is in the habit of "hard." Hard times at work, hard times with children, hard bosses, hard news, hard relationships, hard physical issues, and hard and unexplainable losses. Not trying to be a "kill-joy" here, but it's just the truth of life on Earth.

So, how can we see and experience "hard," accept "hard," and actually embrace "hard" as part of life without cursing it every time it shows up? As hard (no pun intended) as this may sound, I do believe it's possible for those who trust in God.

What scenery do you "stare" at every day? Does the sun shining amidst the clouds bring you hope, joy, and comfort? Or do the clouds become so thick that they confuse, disillusion, and trouble you because they gather around every day, plaguing you when all you want to see is sunshine?

If the second is your go-to response, I'd like to offer a suggestion of viewing your landscape with different lenses. Choose to see "your landscape" through the lenses that expect clouds and be surprised and awed at how they filter the light. Shadows will always be present, but they can allow the beauty of the sun to make the most amazing rays to shine all around. If the sun always shone without the clouds, we'd miss some of the most amazing brilliance of light.

Now I am NOT at all diminishing how difficult it is to live through, go through, and push through the pain that accompanies our "cloud-filled days and seasons." My simple hope here is to provide a different lens, so to speak, as to how we view those challenges and how God can weave them into our story to complete the tapestry of our lives.

God is light in the same way as the sun. He outshines the darkness brought by our clouds/troubles if we draw closer to Him during the stormy seasons.

Time in the Truth

- **John 16:33**
- **2 Corinthians 11:24-33**
- **Romans 5:1-5**
- **Romans 8:18-27; 38, 39**
- **2 Corinthians 1:3-7**
- **2 Corinthians 4:16-18**
- **James 1:2-4**
- **1 Peter 5:6-11**

Mirror Moment

What "hard" are you experiencing now? How can seeing it through a new lens bring peace in the midst of the cloudy season? What ray of sunshine can you see shining around the darkness? Take the pain to the One who can walk you through and discover the beauty of the shadows made by your cloudy days.

Communion with my Creator

Oh Great and Mighty Sun Maker,

Shine in my darkness today. Remind me of Your Presence. Bring to mind Your faithfulness to me in the past so that I can weather this storm. May the brilliance of Your light be brighter in my life than these temporary yet constant cloudy days.

I choose to trust You.

In Jesus' name! Amen

Song Suggestion

Song Title	Artist
Praise You In the Storm	Casting Crowns

Theme

Trials, Troubles

Side Note: Too often we ask for the challenges in our lives to be taken from us instead of asking for the gifts we can receive during them. Today, try not to focus on asking them to be removed, but on the strength, comfort, endurance, and hope in the midst of them.

Discussion Questions following *Clouds Part 2*

1. Do you see your "landscape" as a place of beauty amidst the pain? Or does your beauty and peace depend on a lack of pain? In **John 16:33**, Jesus lets us know our "landscape" will have tribulation, but to remember that HE has overcome the world! How can this truth change your perspective on how you view "hard"?

2. Paul wrote much of the New Testament. He himself endured tremendous challenges, yet after his Damascus Road experience, he never wavered, complained, or questioned God's faithfulness and goodness! What a testimony! Discuss Paul's story together, recognizing his

transformation and his undying devotion to Jesus, even amidst all his trials. Read **2 Corinthians 11:24-33** to get a list of some of the hardships he endured and now shares with the church in Corinth.

3. Embarking on the path to expecting and maybe even embracing hardships, we'll read several passages from Paul's letters to churches across the region. Four of his epistles, or letters, are even believed to have been written from prison (house arrest), yet he never loses hope. Read the passages from **Romans 5:1-5** and spend time dissecting the path from "tribulations" to "hope!"

4. A few chapters over, Paul, in **Romans 8:18-27, 38, and 39** speaks again about facing trials. What can you glean from these verses about the "clouds we face" and how we should respond and react when they seem relentless?

5. Shifting a bit, we are given a glimpse into why we may experience hardships, what we receive during them, and how we can help others. Read **2 Corinthians 1:3-7** and share experiences that drive home Paul's words.

6. We see encouragement during "cloudy" seasons over and over in Scripture. Again in **2 Corinthians 4:16-18**, Paul brings a message of hope. What does this "light affliction," as Paul refers to it, produce in us if we allow it?

7. In God's upside-down economy, how does James say we should embrace the "clouds" in our lives in **James 1:2-4**. And what is our reward, as stated in **verse 12** of the same chapter?

8. Finally, what does Peter say to us about what we should do during trials, and what is the reward we will gain depending on how we face them in **1 Peter 5:6-11**?

9. Listening to the song suggestion "Praise You in the Storm" is a great way to close today's discussion. Then spend some time laying down the emotions you may have concerning the trials in your life, asking specifically for the qualities Paul and others have boldly spoken that should be our response to those challenges if we truly trust in Him.

29. My Mountain Friends

Since we purchased our cabin a few years back, one of the unexpected joys has been to meet several new friends. From joining each other for coffee in the morning to taking walks together, stopping by the road to talk because no one is in a hurry, meeting at our open-air chapel for weekly Sunday service under the trees, sipping wine at each other's cabins in the evenings, laughing as we dance on the deck, sharing meals, and even talking about the latest bear sightings, new friends and friendships flourish. I've discovered whose families are the original owners' children and grandchildren. In our conversations we discover which cabins are passed down, which cabins are being renovated, and which families didn't quite get along with other families. It all seems so quaint and mainly on-the-surface talk until trust is formed and the walls give way to deeper conversations. You begin to discover the pains, the hurts, and the challenges everyone has endured in life, mostly far from our mountain, back home, wherever that may be.

Those deep discussions come from a place of learning to *trust* one another. Trust takes time and a listening ear. The sharing of pain from having lost children tragically, the challenge of infertility, the sadness of rejection from spouses, and the list goes on. You know, the same hurts and pain you've likely experienced, but don't just share with acquaintances. However, you probably need and long to share with a trusted friend who will keep your confidence. I'm honored to be one of the friends that some on our mountain have opened up to. And they, in turn, have listened to me as well.

I know I've covered many areas of pain in our lives in my devotionals, but please bear with me, as I have one more angle on the topic. This one's about true, genuine friendship!

Learning to *listen without fixing,* being *compassionate without judgment,* and *offering peace just by being available* is the framework of a true friend. It's an art we should all master with the Holy Spirit's (the Comforter's) guidance. Take time today to be that trusted friend others can confide in AND find a trusted friend you can share your thoughts and wounds with. The healing will begin once their sadness, and yours, is not in the dark, and you find common ground to be real. The silver lining and glimpses of joy won't be far behind because you've found that a genuine friend is golden.

Time in the Truth

- **Proverbs 17:17**
- **Proverbs 27:6, 9-10;17**
- **Ecclesiastes 4:9-11**
- **Philippians 2:1-11**
- **Galatians 6:2**
- **Ephesians 4:1-6**
- **Hebrews 10:24, 25**
- **James 1:19; 5:16, 17**
- **1 John 1:7**
- **John 15:12-16**

Mirror Moment

Being a good friend takes time and requires emotional and mental capacity to engage by actively being present, listening, and more. Who can you share life with today? Ask someone to coffee or lunch just to listen to their concerns. Ask them if you can pray for them. Without waiting until later, gently ask if you can take their hand (if you are both comfortable with that) and pray a simple prayer over them. They'll likely reciprocate by listening and praying for you as well.

Communion with my Creator

Dear Friend and Great Listener,

Help me learn how to be a friend. Replace any harmful memories of friendships with the truth of what being a friend is truly supposed to be. You've shown us how, through Your life here on Earth! May we discover and uncover those missing qualities that are essential in being a genuine friend. We also want to learn from the Greatest Listener of all time! You listen when we throw everything at You. You remain steadfast and true even when we are not. Learning from the grace You provide us, let us be grace-filled for others. If I'm lacking that godly friendship, give me the courage to reach out and be a friend!

In Jesus' name! Amen

Song Suggestion

Song Title	Artist
Let There Be Light	Hillsong

Theme
Genuine Friendship, Importance of Listening, Trust

Discussion Questions following *My Mountain Friends*

1. Did you have a trusted friend growing up? Talk about that relationship.

2. What is the definition of "friend"? What are the characteristics of a friend? Take a few minutes to make a list and share with one another.

3. Do you find it easy or challenging to find good, trusted friends? Why?

4. What pitfalls can friendships sometimes fall into?

5. Have you ever been hurt by a friend? Or hurt a friend yourself? How can those relationships be mended?

6. What are some of the relationships listed in the Bible that are good AND bad examples of what friendship should look like?

   Hints: **1 Samuel 20; Ruth; 2 Kings 2:9; Job; Acts 9:28; John 15:12-16; Philemon**

7. There are many verses to look up on the topic of friendship. Divide them among your group, or maybe pair up :). Look them up and discuss what your verses say about friendship. Be prepared to share with the group!

   Proverbs 17:17
   Proverbs 27:6, 9-10; 17
   Ecclesiastes 4:9-11
   Philippians 2:1-11
   Galatians 6:2
   Ephesians 4:1-6
   Hebrews 10:24, 25
   James 1:19; 5:16, 17
   1 John 1:7
   John 15:12-16

8. Your belief in someone's potential can change their life. And yours too! Are there any examples of this that you would be willing to share? :)

9. Close by praying for one another, and if time allows, listen to the song suggestion.

Messy Beautiful Friendship by Christine Hoover is a book I highly recommend if you would like to dive deeper into godly friendships. It makes for a wonderful individual read, but it's powerful if read with a group of Jesus-following ladies!

30. Soundless

Silence. Do you ever sit in it for more than five minutes? Can you sit in it for ten?

If one isn't used to silence, it can be deafening at first. We are often scared to be still and quiet. Today, noise, sound, and racket are the norm, keeping us from our own thoughts. Those thoughts that at first scare us away from finding the place of tranquil space. The chaos claims our peace and doesn't provide allowance for us to think, process, or unwind from the knotted mess we sometimes find ourselves in. TV noise, our phones, YouTube, the news, co-workers, bosses, and even our family and friends can and do keep us from experiencing the beauty of silence.

However, the mountain "forces" me into it because of how quiet it usually is. This stillness is a blessing and has taken me places I probably wouldn't have scaled otherwise, including writing this book. Being a parent to five children and having the opportunity to teach for many years, mainly preschool, you can understand being acquainted with quiet wasn't something that came easily, even if I'd wanted to find it.

But in the years since those fun and very loud seasons of my life, the act of finding noiseless spaces has brought clarity to the crossed wires inside my brain. It has also provided my heart a place to heal, to discover peace in the midst of crisis or storms, and even equipped me to handle disturbing news. I certainly haven't perfected how to use silence, but I am committed to practicing until I do.

Quiet doesn't just mean emptying oneself of noise, yet that is an important practice to start with and is always beneficial. Another part of finding quiet is the challenging work of sifting through our thoughts, some wonderful and others not so much—maybe the lies we've been told, the regrets we have, the sadnesses we've encountered. The opposite is also true. Like wonderful memories, finding treasures we'd not thought of in a long time, or sitting in a place of gratefulness. Often tears ensue during this practice. Both sad ones and happy ones. Let them flow. The more practiced we become at finding our soundless space and using it wisely, the more we need it and have trouble thriving without it, as it brings rest to our souls and clarity to our tomorrows.

After sitting in stillness, our ears become sharpened and more adept at listening. Listen for what, you might ask? First, we may just need to listen to our heartbeat and our breath, practicing that stillness. Long, deep cleansing breaths that prepare us for the still quiet voice from Heaven, whose name is above all names and has a message for us to hear on a daily basis.

Don't be afraid of the silence. As a believer in the Holy Spirit's work in our lives, He will be the guiding Voice you'll begin to hear. I can't really explain what that means. But it happens, and when it does, you'll know, and you'll welcome it as a friend you didn't know you needed but now can't live without.

Time in the Truth

- **Isaiah 26:3, 4**
- **Ecclesiastes 9:17**
- **Psalm 1:2; 77:12; 145:5**
- **Philippians 4:7, 8**
- **Psalm 23:2-4; 46:10; 62:5**
- **1 Corinthians 2:12**
- **Romans 12:2**
- **Mark 1:35**
- **Luke 5:15, 16; 6:12**

Mirror Moment

Find your soundless space.
Then breathe, big deep breaths.
Finally begin to truly listen.
Then ask yourself what you're beginning to learn.

Communion with my Creator

Devote today's prayer to listening.

Holy Spirit, speak to me as I sit now in this silence. I commit to truly attending and attuning my ear to You to discover what You want me to hear.

Amen

Song Suggestion

Song Title	Artist
None But Jesus	Hillsong United

Theme

Listening, Embracing Silence

Discussion Questions following *Soundless*

1. When you were in school, could you study and read with sound or music, or did your brain require silence?

2. Do you like silence? Why or why not? What are some distractions that keep us from enjoying silence? Why are we sometimes afraid of it? Our minds often "run wild" when we are silent... Read the truth in **Isaiah 26:3, 4** to remind ourselves of the benefit of trusting God.

3. **Ecclesiastes 9:17** speaks of words heard "in calm." Share how settings have an impact on our ability to listen. What are some things that can help our ability to hear from God? Consider stopping here to listen to the song suggestion, "None But Jesus."

4. Sometimes we need to empty our heads of sound altogether and sit in silence. There is a huge benefit to this practice. However, a wonderful companion to the quiet stillness, and one that will greatly increase the benefit of our quiet posture, is meditation. Meditating on the Word of God. Share your experiences with this practice, and then read the following verses that express how important this exercise is: **Psalm 1:2; 77:12; 145:5; Philippians 4:7, 8.**

5. Communicating with our soul and spirit requires stillness. **Read 1 Corinthians 2:12** and **Romans 12:2**. What do we gain from listening to the Holy Spirit?

6. Likely, the verses in the following Psalms are familiar to you. Read them again with the idea of silence and stillness in mind. How does God intend for us to learn from him? **Psalm 23:2-4; 46:10; 62:5.**

7. What did Jesus often do to model listening to His Father? Verses to jog your memory: **Mark 1:35; Luke 5:16; Luke 6:12.**

8. We were created to be in a relationship with God. We were NOT created to do life alone or to always be the one to talk at God. Relationships like that never last. Let's commit to shifting how we pray and spend more time creating space to listen when we pray. **Psalm 42:1, 2** is a beautiful illustration of how our souls were designed to need Him!

9. For further study, if time allows, read the story of Elijah in **1 Kings 1:1-18** and discover how God speaks to Elijah.

10. Spend the last few minutes of your time together simply asking the Holy Spirit to begin speaking to you personally. Your group could end in silence, and everyone could leave quietly, allowing everyone to stay as long as needed in order to listen.

31. Renovations Part 1: Taking Inventory and Decluttering

I've shared with you that when we first bought our cabin, it was mainly for the view from our deck! You're probably thinking, *Enough of that...*

We also saw great potential for what the inside could be if we worked at it. The cabin had been built in 1983 but had not been updated since then. We bought it in 2018 with all the original furniture, decor, kitchen supplies, old canned goods... You get the picture. The outdated 1980s paneling and even a not-so-real stone fireplace. We could tell there was so much love that had gone into the building of it, yet it was in dire need of a "facelift." *There was work to be done.* So, we hired a contractor and worked with him to completely take things down to the studs that were firmly in place and to rebuild. The furnishings and almost everything inside were sold at the Angel's Attic I mentioned in an earlier devotional. It was a time of weeding out and discovering the possibilities of creating a space that was right for us and those loved ones who have stayed and will stay here.

How quickly can *our* lives become cluttered, dusty, and unmanageable if we aren't careful to take inventory of what we should hang on to and what we should let go of?

Take inventory, you ask? Yikes. In a home, it's easy to put things in drawers or way back in closets, or even storage buildings, in case we "might ever need or use them again." The same goes for our lives. We tend to shove back or hang onto things we should have long ago parted with. What have we shoved back so deeply we barely remember it being there? We have gotten so used to pushing this or that to one side or another without dealing with it, so it distracts and keeps us from being open to fully living in our present world, offering freedom from the outdated and unnecessary "remains"?

Don't get me wrong. Sentimental is good and worthy to hold onto. Outdated canned goods, not so much. So go for good, meaningful memories, vs. harsh, sometimes traumatic ones, that haunt and impose upon our present and future selves. I can't speak to each of the "remains" you may have, but I do know they require our work of sorting through and, unfortunately, getting up close and personal with in order to discover the possibilities of creating the space necessary for God to do in our life what He wants for us now. The space that provides purpose and peace in the present and future.

If there is any remotely relatable thought that comes to mind while reading this devotional, please stop and use the resources necessary and available to you so that your life, present and future, can resemble a cozy mountain retreat inside, with a view of the mountains! Don't give up. Begin today.

It is attainable, one step at a time.

Time in the Truth

- **Psalm 51:1-10**
- **2 Corinthians 7:1**
- **Ephesians 4:30-32**
- **James 1:21-25**
- **Titus 3:4-7**
- **Hebrews 12:1-3**

Mirror Moment

What are you holding on to that you need to let go? Is it grudges, reputation, image, secret failures, dreams and goals, or rights? What is holding you back that needs shedding and shredding? Do you have unresolved anger? Have you held onto hurts or become bitter? What relationship is unhealthy? What lies do you continue to believe that are not true? Where are you not right with your vertical relationship with Heavenly Father?

Take the time needed to examine, take inventory, and begin the process of cleaning out, letting go, and embracing the importance of the eternal, and the life you know is available, and you should be living now.

Communion with my Creator

Oh, Renovator of My Heart,

As I begin to take inventory of myself, gently, yet firmly reveal the areas I need to become aware of so I can deal wisely with them. Guide my next steps in handling the parts of me that require some attention. I know I can trust You with my hidden places as I start the hard journey of letting go and surrendering, in order that no one and nothing competes with Your throne in my heart.

In Jesus' name! Amen

Song Suggestion

Song Title	Artist
Graves Into Gardens	Elevation Worship

Theme

Taking Inventory and Decluttering :)

Discussion Questions following *Renovations Part 1: Taking Inventory and Decluttering*

1. Tell about a time when you inventoried and decluttered a closet.

   Check out the name of this devotional. What is the difference between inventory and decluttering? Why are they each important? What happens if decluttering comes before inventorying, both in a closet and in our lives?

2. How does taking inventory reveal what needs to be decluttered? Read the questions in the mirror moment, taking as much time as your group would like in reflecting on them. As you begin this self-evaluation, how does God's Word encourage you in this process? Read **Psalm 51:1-10** and **2 Corinthians 7:1** to begin this discussion.

3. What place might sadness or regret have in this process? How might we all deal with it? Does the sadness, regret, or reminder of "items" we've held onto so long make us grip tighter? How can these emotions become part of the letting go, as well as begin the healing process?

4. Read and discuss this acrostic, which may help in setting your "I and D" in motion!   "I. C.a.l.m.!"

5. *Identify* those things in your life that need to be decluttered. What was their purpose (if they ever had one)? Have they fulfilled their purpose? And if so, begin the process of letting go. Be specific.

6. *Choose* how to deal with "said memory." What does this look like for you and your memory or issue? Some of the solutions could be fervent prayer, sharing with a trusted, balanced friend, coming to a place of forgiveness (for yourself and the other party)

    Let the truth in **Titus 3:4-7** remind you that it is the work of the Holy Spirit and the mercy of God doing the work of cleansing/decluttering! You are NOT alone in the process.

7. *Address* it/them NOW. Be specific by naming and speaking aloud the "outdated unnecessary remains." Doing so keeps us from being vague and pushing them even further into our cluttered existence.

    Read the truth from **Ephesians 4:30-32** to guide and bring wisdom to this discussion.

8. *Leave* it. Once you have dealt with "said issues" that need to be uprooted and thrown away, don't pick them back up. Truly surrender. This may take time, depending on how old the "canned goods" in our lives are, and several attempts, but don't give up, even if it takes 1,000 tries. What does it actually look like to constantly lay it down?

    Read the truth in **James 1:21-25** as you ask God for wisdom in laying down your clutter.

9. *Move* Forward. After inventorying and decluttering, it's time to move on. Look ahead. Whether that is mended relationships, a healthy boundary, a new career, a move to a new city... a life change of some sort, however big or small!

    Hebrews 12:1-3 is an amazing bit of Scripture that will bring encouragement. (If you need to read some of **Hebrews 11** in order to get context before discussing, please do so.) What phrases stand out in these verses that help with the process of moving forward?

    Consider reading **Hebrews 12** in the Amplified Version, spending time on what Jesus endured and what his example can and should mean to our lives.

10. As always, don't forget to pray, and if time allows, listen to the powerful song suggestion.

32. Renovations Part 2: Adding Windows

Let the light in! Darkness hides, but light reveals. Darkness lies, but light sheds truth. Darkness belittles, but light encourages. Darkness questions our existence, but light answers with resounding worth. Darkness saddens, but light brings joy. Darkness shames shamelessly, but light frees. Darkness is where secrets fester, but light comes with surrender. Before I get too carried away, I should give my metaphor a chance so you can catch up with the list my brain just ran away with.

Our cabin was well built but was lacking light. The studs were solid, yet the solid foundation and walls kept the air and light flow from fulfilling its purpose of cleansing the air, and allowing for the natural brilliance to shine through.

Windows matter, in a home as well as in our lives. They are crucial to health. Without air flow and light, we can't survive, much less thrive. So, the first thing we did when we bought our cabin was figure out how many more windows we could install to provide the most air and light possible without damaging the strong structure. We've been able to do so in our cabin, bringing fresh air and natural light into our space.

Our lives are really no different.

In our lives, if we allow walls to enclose us, they can squelch us. Darkness often masks as comforting and dresses up as safe. It provides the illusion of a warm blanket yet suffocates slowly. **WARNING:** Darkness is neither comforting or safe and will stifle growth. It is a liar and a deceiver, playing on our tender emotions, keeping us from bouldering through to get to the fresh air and light God so desires for our lives.

Until a few years ago, I couldn't personally relate much to anything I'm writing here; but fairly recent experiences have led to a much clearer understanding of how existent darkness is pure and

← AFTER ADDING NUMEROUS WINDOWS OUR SPACE
  BECAME BRIGHT AND FULL OF LIGHT!

insidious evil, and how so many people unfortunately can't, and will never, push through to find the light in which they should and were created to live.

Light IS life. Don't be afraid to face the darkness. Then call on the name of Light itself, Jesus, and fight like crazy to reach a place of fresh air, light, and freedom! Freedom, and living in the light is worth it, and available if you're willing to do the work! Just like the previous devotional on inventorying and decluttering, find a good counselor, seek out a good friend to be a confidant in the process, and don't give up!

Windows Matter!

Side note: This specific devotional may resemble the previous one and even some of the ones before. However, take the time to dig a little deeper into the concept of Light in Scripture and see where God has a lesson for you!

Time in the Truth

- **Psalm 27:1**
- **Psalm 36:9**
- **Psalm 119:105**
- **John 1:4, 5; 3:19-21; 8:12; 12:35, 36**
- **1 John 1:5-10**
- **Matthew 5:14-16**

Mirror Moment

Lord, where am I comfortable in the darkness? Where have I neglected to allow you to shine your light or withheld your presence from shining? Re-read the first paragraph of the devotional and pinpoint which sentence best relates to your darkness/light story. Take whatever you've kept neatly hidden, and offer it to God, so His light can pierce and illuminate it with light! Let the floodlights begin to bring redemption. And then, read the last paragraph of the devo and DO IT! God, along with a confidant or a wise counselor, makes surrender, healing, and emerging victory in the light possible!

Communion with my Creator

Oh, Darkness Crusher and Light Flooder!

Darknesshasnoplaceinmylife.Darkness,youarenolongerwelcome. I name my darkness, which is _____ and I claim victory in the Light!

I know it's easier said than done. And, because I can easily hide again, along with naming what is in my darkness, I SURRENDER my dark, hidden, secret places to You.

Take me in my surrendered state to the foot of Your cross and keep me in my kneeled posture, until I am fully and completely surrendered. Let the Light You put in me shine brightly so as to bring You Glory and Praise!

In Jesus' name! Amen

Song Suggestion

Song Title	Artist
Let the Light In	Cody Carnes

Theme

Dispelling Darkness and Sin, The Importance and

Power Living in the Light, Masks We Wear

Discussion Questions following *Renovations Part 2: Adding Windows*

1. What happens when the light is turned on in a dark room? In the south, where I grew up—New Orleans, to be exact— the roaches scattered! Not knowing what is there, hidden in the darkness, can offer an extremely false sense of safety. What false sense of safety have you experienced until you or someone else 'turned on the light'?

2. How can you relate to the dark/light metaphor? What stood out to you in the body of today's devotional? You may want to focus on/reread the first paragraph to help you and your group share more deeply.

3. Little children and maybe even some adults are truly afraid of the dark. There are good causes for this. Fear can be demoralizing, debilitating, and paralyzing because of what happens in the dark. **Psalm 27:1** and **Psalm 119:105** are wonderful verses to begin our discussion on the distinct difference between darkness and light, as well as the importance of light and where it actually comes from. Share your thoughts.

4. God was referred to as Light at least 36 times in Scripture. That is how vital Light is to Him. Read the verses below, mainly from the apostle John's gospel (mostly Jesus' exact words) and one of his epistles, drawing from them the significance of light! Use the following questions to understand these verses more fully.

    John 1:4, 5; 3:19-21; 8:12; 12:35, 36; 1 John 1:5-10

    a. Can darkness and light coexist? Why or why not?

    b. The words 'life and light' are often seen together. Why do you think that is? What are the opposites of 'life and light', and how does this realization bring us to the place of wanting to stay in the light?

    c. So much of spiritual warfare takes place in the dark. How can exposing the darkness to His Light bring victory to your dark places?

    d. Where have you experienced true Light in an area of your life that used to be filled with darkness?

5. How does wearing "masks" betray where God wants you to experience His Light?

   Why do people wear them? Pinpoint the masks we often wear to keep us in darkness. Be honest about the ones you have, or are, prone to putting on.

   Some of the masks we wear could include: the Victim Mask, Humor Mask, Avoidant Mask, "I'm Fine" Mask, Controlling Mask, People Pleasing Mask, Overachieving Mask, Self-Bashing Mask

6. **Matthew 5:14-16** refers to us as Light! Are you comfortable with what is proclaimed here? How are these verses an extension of Jesus being the Light?

7. Finally, use the song suggestion, **Psalm 36:9**, and the prayer to close out your time together. Leave today determined to add windows to your life, letting in the air and the Light of the World!

33. Renovations Part 3: Long Hauls

Decluttering, taking inventory, and adding windows were key steps in building our refuge in the mountains once we purchased our cabin. Hard work for sure! But then came the next phase. Refinishing, redecorating, restocking, reorganizing, and refurnishing. All the "RE's" that are necessary to find peace in the "completion."

Our main residence is about 4.5 hours from our mountain respite. Once the process got to that point, we then had the responsibility of moving forward, which meant countless trips of hauling EVERYTHING those 4+ hours up!! This included everything from simple necessities like kitchen utensils and bath towels to flooring, beds, mattresses, an oven, a refrigerator, toilets, shower doors... You name it, we hauled it! And we did it with the "end" in sight. We did it because we knew the outcome would be worth it! We did it mostly with joy, keeping in mind the space we were creating to relax and unwind and provide the same for those we love! In hindsight, we probably could have had some of those items delivered, but that's a devotional for another time.

We had a goal, and we did not lose sight of it. That is also a key to accomplishing things in our lives. Having attainable goals, with attainable steps! Key word: attainable. One step at a time!

I call them "sticky note" progress. Even though sticky notes are small and may seem insignificant, one hundred sticky note steps (or even five or ten), one by one, provide the things dreams are made of! So, one haul a month or one sticky note at a time, progress is made to bring about completion! Yours included!

The "RE's" I spoke of earlier will find their way to new "RE's." Once those are faced, challenged, and climbed, new ones emerge. Those of reclaim, resolve, refine, and reflect are possible! What a place of peace they have been to us in the cabin remodel, but they are most assuredly worth it when they play out in our lives.

← ABOUT AN HOUR FROM THE CABIN WE BEGIN TO SEE THE MOUNTAINS DIRECTLY OUT IN FRONT. THE JOURNEY IS WORTH IT EVERY TIME.

We completed our hauling after about 10+ trips, which amounted to well over one hundred hours of work. On top of travel (loading, hauling, unloading), there were over 4,300 miles of driving, which included the trip there and back, plus gas. I didn't do 'that' math... But what I can tell you is **it's all been worth it**. And it will be in your life as well.

My message to you today is, don't give up, just like I've said in Devotionals, Renovations 1 and 2.

Your "RE" is attainable.

Time in the Truth

- **2 Corinthians 5:14-21**
- **Ezekiel 36:26**
- **Isaiah 43:18-19**
- **Colossians 3:9-10**
- **Philippians 1:6**
- **Galatians 2:20**

Mirror Moment

The prefix "re" means "anew!" Don't we all want to experience an "anew" in our lives in one area or another? What do you need to do to get there? After you've "decluttered" and "taken inventory" and "added windows," as you read about in the previous devotionals, now you're at the point to move ahead to experience **renewal!** Ask God where and what that means in your own life during this particular season! Don't just dream about it coming true. Claim it and live it out!

Communion with my Creator

Oh God of the New!

You make all things new! I believe it! You believe in me and in the newness of life! You are able, and I am willing, for You to take my old way of thinking, my harmful habits, and my sinful ways and turn them into newness of thinking, of life-giving and life-launching! Help me today to take one step (one sticky note) at a time, making each step with You, and clearing my path to the place You have for me! I choose to reclaim and restore what the locust has eaten! And to live untethered with Your purpose for me!

In Jesus' name! Amen

Song Suggestion

Song Title	Artist
I've Witnessed It	Melodie Malone and Passion

Theme

Do-Overs, New Beginnings

Discussion Questions following *Renovations Part 3: Long Hauls*

1. Have you ever done renovations in a home you've owned? What were some of the lessons learned through that process? What qualities were needed to get the job done?

2. Read **2 Corinthians 5:14-21**. How do these verses speak to the renovations that need to take place in our hearts, and how do they relate to all the 're' words listed in the first paragraph of the devotional? Hint: How does the finishing of a cabin or home remodel resemble what should take place in our lives to be reconciled to God and to see a bright and promising future?

3. Time for testimonies! Find one or two someones in your group (hopefully prior to your group study) to read and study Part 3 and the verses. Allow them to share their personal testimonies in regard to their "re"-stories!!! Allow for about five or six minutes each, maybe with some discussion and encouragement after each one.

4. If time allows, open the floor for others to share as well.

5. For some further Scripture references on today's topic check out the following verses: **Ezekiel 36:26; Isaiah 43:18-19; Colossians 3:9-10; Philippians 1:6**

6. Personalize **Galatians 2:20** for each one in your group. How is this verse critical in the 'living out' of our newly remodeled heart and soul?

7. Close in prayer and listen to the song suggestion!

34. Renovations Part 4: UP-Keep

This could be the hardest of all when it comes to cabin renovations. There is an excitement during Parts 1-3. As **challenging** as they might be, there is still a goal in mind and a completion we can take pride in! Yet the upkeep of our home, and our lives for that matter, depends on our diligence to stay sharpened and keep things in tip-top shape. Or sliding backwards can and does occur.

Once our cabin was "completed," we began to truly enjoy it and the amazing scenery and all that the mountains have to offer. It's been sweetly rejuvenating, as expressed in many earlier devotionals. However, there is the condition of too much comfort that can lead to *complacency*, which leads to things breaking down, needing service, running low, becoming dingy, and so forth. This can certainly happen in the cabin with such things as sanding and staining the deck, sealing leaks from the wood-burning stove, replacing water filters, replacing heaters... and the list goes on. But it's highly probable to happen in our lives and relationships as well if we don't stay aware and vigilant.

Being unaware of how complacency and falling into excess comfort and satisfaction can tarnish our newly found place of freedom and peace and lead to diminishing our health, stopping our growth, and extinguishing our enthusiasm for change and possibilities. Ultimately leading us onto dangerous slippery slopes and disrepair. *However, awareness of the same can lead us to renewed personal growth and sharpened and vibrant relationships.*

I'm certainly not against enjoying hard work completed and taking time to bask in the accomplishments made. But, if we only commit to completing a goal and don't spend time nurturing and polishing it in the days, weeks, and years to come, stagnancy and even a spirit of negativity and resentment can easily occur.

← IT'S ME, HAPPY ABOUT THE PROGRESS WE ARE MAKING IN OUR RENOVATIONS.

All of this speaks to our own growth, our horizontal relationships, AND certainly our vertical one with God as well.

Guard against complacency, and keep up the renovations for a lifetime!

Time in the Truth

- **Proverbs 1:32**
- **Isaiah 37:29**
- **Jeremiah 29:11**
- **Zephaniah 1:12**
- **Matthew 25:1-13**
- **1 Thessalonians 5:1-11**
- **Revelation 3:14-22**

Mirror Moment

What area in your life has fallen into disrepair? Where have you experienced complacency? Stopping to think of where you are negative or pessimistic will sometimes help you to pinpoint those areas that need some upkeep! What steps can you take to polish up your once-shiny remodel?

Also, what relationships have fallen into the category of complacency for you? Ponder why, and what part you've played in this present situation. What practical steps can you take to nourish these relationships and restore them to a place of beauty, including your relationship with God?

Communion with my Creator

Dear Master Carpenter,

You know full well the pitfalls of not keeping up with repairs, both with physical structures and, more importantly, when it comes to staying sharpened ourselves. Bring awareness to me of where I have left areas of my life unattended only to have them fall into disarray. Where messes have taken over what used to be beautiful. Give me the boldness to take the steps necessary to once again bring the shine back into my life and my relationships.

In Jesus' name! Amen

Song Suggestions

Song Title	Artist
In Christ Alone	Shane & Shane
Set a Fire	Will Reagan, United Pursuit

Theme

Fighting Complacency

Discussion Questions following *Renovations Part 4: UP-Keep*

1. Was there a time in your life when you were completely satisfied with an accomplishment? How did it feel to have arrived? How did it affect your life?

2. I don't think there is anything wrong with celebrating the success of a job well done, or a project completed. However, what seems to happen in the days, weeks, and years after that achievement is complete?

3. Scripture speaks loud and clear throughout about those who are complacent. Listen to the song suggestion, "Set a Fire," by Will Reagan. Then read the verses in the following questions with humility, to disclose areas in your own life that need to be reignited.

4. What quality of a person is evident in a life marked by complacency in **Proverbs 1:32**, and what is their demise? Have you ever found yourself in these categories in any area of your life? Are there any specific examples of the outcomes of this in your own life?

5. **Isaiah 37:29** is quite a graphic depiction of what God does to those who are complacent. But how does this also show God's desire for us to return to Him?

6. What warning are we given in **Zephaniah 1:12** for those He finds complacent? What word is used in place of 'complacent' in this verse? Discuss for a bit the meaning of the phrase 'stagnant in spirit' when it comes to both water and our lives.

7. Study Jesus' parable in **Matthew 25:1-13** and discuss further the dangers of not being prepared and the benefits of the opposite! How does 1 Thessalonians 5:1-11 speak to the same? What further wisdom can be gleaned from it?

8. One of the clearest pictures of what complacency, dullness, and stagnation can lead to is found in the letter to the Laodicean church in **Revelation 3:14-22**. Read it with honesty, discovering how **verses 18-22** provide the action needed to be taken, and the hope God makes available, for those wallowing in "lukewarm-ness."

9. Choose one area of your life where you believe laziness has become your norm. Share it with your group. Map out a plan to be accountable to each other as you get out of that rut!! And end with the communion prayer and the hymn suggestion.

35. Loss Part 1:
Fire

The blessing of a place to get away, rest, and relax has been beyond anything we ever dreamed of. Each time we drive to our place, we pinch ourselves and ask if it's real. The winter we renovated was one of the driest on record, and shortly after completing the renovations, a fire ignited nearby that destroyed 39,000 acres. We realized that all the work, time, effort, and resources we'd spent and labored for could be destroyed before even enjoying a single summer here. We are grateful that it did not happen. But just a few short years later, another fire that destroyed 400,000 acres came along not too far from us and did even more damage. Some very dear friends and many, many others lost everything. It can happen in the blink of an eye, and we have no control.

The same holds true for our lives. None of us is promised tomorrow, or even the next hour. When events in our lives remind us of this truth, we are brought face-to-face with our mortality. I am sure you can think of some events of your own, or those close to you, that have brought the glaring reality of the fragility of life into focus. What change occurs inside us when we realize the brevity of our time on Earth? Maybe we can begin to be more grateful for what we have. Perhaps we stop complaining about "first world problems," possibly we begin to take better care of ourselves, and hopefully we work to mend broken relationships. These are all great responses to close calls. They can make a tremendous difference in how we live and how we will be remembered.

However, keeping the momentum of those transformational shifts in our present and future mindset can be, and usually is, hard to do. As human nature has it, we easily slip back into old habits or routines because of our short memories.

So, what can we do to remind ourselves to stay the course and continue to live as if we don't have control of our tomorrows? One of my "secrets" to this is remembering we have a legacy to pass on. Remembering our legacy should cause us to pause before we respond, count before we speak, and pray before we react. Who will be the recipient of your legacy? And how important is it to provide them with your life well lived? *How we live our "todays" matters for others' "tomorrows."*

Even with the right mindset and motivation, this can be mighty challenging, given the state of affairs in a fallen world. But IF we believe in a Higher Power that transcends our mortal bodies, knowing He is more than able to fill in the places this life has failed us, including losing everything by fire, **we can remain steadfast and full of hope.**

When we know our final destiny and who we belong to, there should be a shift in our minds and hearts that remains resolute. The constant of an Everlasting God, who promises us an inheritance as His heirs, who we can draw strength from now, and who has sent His Spirit to guide us while we remain on this planet living this tightrope life, should be enough. Enough, no matter what. Enough if we lose it all. Enough if we haven't experienced what we thought we should or were deserving of. Enough because we were created in His image, imprinted with the image of the King of Kings and Lord of Lords.

You are enough. And He is "Our Enough."

My friends who lost everything due to the fires gave themselves time to grieve their loss. But they also recognized we are all fragile, with no control over our stuff or our lives. They committed to continue to live grateful, thankful, full lives again.

What a legacy testimony that will live on. Our legacy matters!

Time in the Truth

- **Job 13:15, 19:25-27**
- **Lamentations 3:22-24**
- **Psalm 73:26; 118:1-6; 136**
- **Romans 5:3-5**
- **1 Peter 1:3-9**
- **Hebrews 6:19, 20**

Mirror Moment

God's Promises have a way of bringing reassurance to our weary souls in times of loss. They can sometimes remind us of our frailty. However, when we recognize the incredible strength and hope we have as we rely on Him and His Promises, we are reassured that He is enough! Study God's Promises and be encouraged through your losses.

Take time today to meditate on **Romans 5:3-5** and how these verses reinforce your legacy. Allow the pattern in these verses to take root in your core.

Communion with my Creator

Dear Hope Giver,

I choose to praise You in the midst of my loss. You are the Everlasting Father, the Great Promise Giver and Keeper. Even if I lose everything, including my life, YOU are enough. May these words I speak today become how I live until I breathe my last breath, so the legacy I leave points directly to You and lives on in the dear ones I've shared life with.

In Jesus' name! Amen

Song Suggestions

Song Title	Artist
Tis So Sweet to Trust in Jesus	Casting Crowns
Jireh	Elevation Worship
More Than Enough	Kari Jobe

Theme
Loss, Embracing Every Day, Only One Constant

Discussion Questions following *Loss Part 1: Fire*

1. What event in your life has made you realize your mortality?

2. Have you experienced the feeling of being in control of your life one minute and not the next? What has helped you when you have had the feeling of being totally out of control?

3. The book of Job is a perfect example of one who lost it all and was severely tested. **Job 13:15** says, "Though he slay me, I will hope in Him." How hard must this statement have been for Job to proclaim, knowing what he was living through? Follow up this discussion by reading **Job 19:25-27**.

   Consider the phrase in the devotional "He is our Enough." How does believing and trusting this phrase, and Job's outlook, change the equation of our lives when "fires" seem to destroy everything?

4. **Lamentations 3:22-24** has provided so much comfort and reassurance in my life over the years. How do these verses speak the same comfort and strength to you?

5. How does proclaiming God's enduring love, goodness, and faithfulness in times of such pain bring about hope? Read these verses and be reminded: **Psalm 73:26; 118:1-6; 136**.

6. As hard as it is to be joyful in times like these, consider for a moment the lessons you have learned and the growth that takes place after a "fire." Read **Romans 5:3-5** to add to your discussion and to offer hope when the loss feels impossible.

7. What are the benefits described of going through suffering in **1 Peter 1:3-9**? How easy, or challenging, is the joy described here for you to attain? **Hebrews 6:19, 20** gives us the reason hope is even possible in our losses. Read those verses and pick out key words used by the author to assure us God has not left or forsaken us!

8. Consider the truth that Jesus is our ENOUGH, that we have no control over our destiny, and that we aren't promised tomorrow. How will you tangibly remind yourself of this every day and live life with the hope, joy, and peace we read about today?

9. Close in prayer, and by listening to one or more of the song suggestions.

36. Loss Part 2: Loving, Losing, Lamenting, and Living Onward

When we love, we risk. When we love, we allow ourselves to be vulnerable. When we love, we open ourselves up to feel. When we love, we sometimes have to brace ourselves for hits. When we love, we also shouldn't be surprised if there is push back. So is loving actually worth it?

I've also found that when we allow love to flow, we find purpose. And when we love, we usually receive love in return.

Let's take a peek into discovering this complicated concept and answering the question, "Is loving deeply worth it?"

Listening to stories of love, love lost, and living onward, and some who have loved and are still trapped in their grief, inspired today's words.

Several of my mountain friends have tragic stories of those who have loved deeply and then lost. Several of these losses were their children. However, most have found resiliency in life beyond, and alongside, the pain. Words can't do it justice, devotionals can't explain it, and even though Scripture can soften it or make it bearable, it too can't take away the pain of this type of devastating loss.

Several of these lovely people have had the courage to push through, their strong resolve fighting through the grief, which has allowed many of them to live onward. Listening as they share their stories, I'm amazed at just how fresh their pain still seems even though many of these losses happened twenty or thirty years ago, when their children were quite young. So, it is not that they are "over their loss," for that would be impossible, but they have chosen to live life after their loss and decided that their loss doesn't have to define them but instead is a part of the fabric of who they've become. They also recognize and have expressed that having peace and joy does not diminish the constant ache of their loss. Realizing that both

← PSALM 121:1, 2 "I WILL RAISE MY EYES TO THE MOUNTAINS;
FROM WHERE DOES MY HELP COME? MY HELP COMES FROM THE LORD,
WHO MADE HEAVEN AND EARTH."

157

emotions can live simultaneously within themselves has made them more than conquerors in this life, which is, and always will be, full of joy and sorrow together.

Another lesson I've learned about this painful ache of grief is how important it is to keep the memories of their loved ones alive by talking about them and actively doing things to keep their memories alive! It has been an honor to be a listening ear!

Sadly, there is also another mountain friend who lost her husband early in their marriage. She has struggled with the concept of living onward, afraid that allowing herself joy will lessen the love she had for her husband. She confided in me that she takes her husband's ashes with her wherever she goes. That was twelve years ago. This saddens me greatly, and I have prayed she would find peace alongside her grief.

I am well aware that everyone grieves differently, and we all experience loss in varying ways. The grief timeline is quite personal and never linear. I respect everyone's unique journey towards finding the balance to embrace the good and bad life throws our way.

So, to answer my own question I posed earlier, "Is loving deeply worth it?" I absolutely believe it is. But I've wrestled with how to frame my thoughts to finish this devotional. The answer just so happened to come a couple of years after first writing this lesson. One of my dear friends, who lost his teenage son years ago, lost his entire home to a fire just a few months back, and now his wife is struggling with and battling a sudden major health issue. He said with tears in his eyes but a genuine smile on his face, "We've lived a full life in every season, and all the memories are precious. Now it's time for a new season." He and his wife's resiliency is a testament to what it means to fully embrace both joy and sadness. Loving deeply is worth it.

Time in the Truth

I have used these Scriptures about finding comfort on several other occasions throughout this book. But after writing this devotional, I find that we need them once again. Ask God to help you see them with fresh eyes as you embrace the solace and peace they can bring.

- Job 42:1-6
- Psalm 23
- Isaiah 41:10
- Lamentations 3:19-26
- Habakkuk 3: 17-19
- 2 Corinthians 1:2-7
- Matthew 5:4; 11:28, 29
- 1 Peter 5:7

Mirror Moment

You may not have to think long to find a personal story of love and loss. Whether it is through death, betrayal, or rejection, young person or old. I would suggest you find one of the passages above and meditate on it as you sit silently, asking God to gently wrap His loving, everlasting arms around you.

I would also suggest you read over the five stages of grief, discover the stage you're in, and do the hard work of pushing through it. Ask God to show you how. Take baby steps to address your individual pain. And as I always encourage, consider seeking out a sober-minded friend and/or therapist who can help you.

What I don't want is for this devotional to fall on deaf ears, rationalizing or staying stuck where you are and not living this life to the fullest.

Be willing to trust again, open up again, and love again. Yes, I do believe it's worth it.

Communion with my Creator

Oh, Designer of All Emotions,

You alone created them all, and they are all helpful in this life at one time or another. Bring clarity to my pain, and show me the way to stay the course so I may experience life to the fullest. And if I'm still not convinced You understand me, remind me of the grief You must've felt sacrificing Your own Son to die on the cross to take our place. This idea is beyond my imagination.

Bring me the comfort needed that will eventually lead me to a place of hope for tomorrow.

In Jesus' name! Amen

Song Suggestions

Song Title	Artist
Heaven Song	Phil Wickham
Held	Natalie Grant
It is Well	Audrey Assad

Theme

Loss, Grief

Discussion Questions following *Loss Part 2: Loving, Losing, Lamenting, and Living Forward*

1. What does loving have to do with being vulnerable? How has this played out in your life?

2. Define grief. Talk about the aspects of grief. If anyone cares to share their grief stories, allow time for this.

3. Loss of life can come in the form of death, of course, but it can also come in the form of rejection and abandonment, such as divorce. How do these forms of loss bring added challenges to the loss equation?

4. We will once again check in with Job today. **Job 42:1-6** is Job's confession of God's sovereignty over his sadness. It takes Job a long time to arrive at this point in his grief process. What can you glean from reading his words?

5. God is the God of comfort. The following sets of verses provide support and strength for the weary griever. Read them, and share how they can, and possibly have, brought freedom from the pain you've experienced in your own life. Remember to read them with fresh eyes, as I know we have read them in past devotionals.

   a. **Psalm 23** In seasons of great sadness, how does seeing Jesus as our Shepherd bring comfort?

   b. **Isaiah 41:10** Be filled with the strength God can provide.

   c. **Lamentations 3:1-26** By beginning at verse 1, it allows a full picture of the misery and grief Jeremiah goes through before declaring the hope he finds in God's mercy! How can you relate to this?

   d. **Habakkuk 3:17-19** Take note of the "Even if" statements. Now, take a few minutes to write out some of your own "even if" statements to God. This may be a hard exercise, but I believe it will help remind you of the greatness of God.

   e. **Matthew 5:4; 11:28, 29** Read these passages and take time to discuss how they can relieve the heavy burden of loss.

6. **2 Corinthians 1:2-7** paints a picture of how receiving God's comfort allows that same comfort to flow from us to others. Isn't that just like God to make our suffering part of our testimony in order to help others going through some of the same losses!? If there is time, please share how this has been true in your life.

7. Using one of the suggested songs and the prayer provided, pray directly over anyone who is grieving a loss. **1 Peter 5:7**: Close with this verse using the Amplified Version as you prayerfully consider how you will live onward.

37. Love Across the Decades

Several years ago, I became a grandmother, fondly known as Lolli. The love I had and still have for that grandchild and several grandchildren since has become one of the most amazing joys in my life. I try to tuck away as many memories as I can as they grow.

My father is also still on this side of Heaven, and the joy he continues to bring to us all is truly a blessing.

But when you bring these two precious individuals together, the love they share is magical to watch. They were born ninety-two years apart, but that did not stop them then, or now, from sharing a special bond. One of those memories I've tucked close to my heart is of the two of them together up at our cabin. My dad at the time was ninety-three years young, and my grandson was eighteen months old. They both recognized the importance of living in the moment, embracing the simplicity of being together. One who had lived so much life that he knew the value of every minute and therefore treasured each one he had the privilege of sharing with his great-grandson. And the other, soaking up the attention his Paw Paw was so willing to give him. Neither one worried about a thing beyond that precious moment in time.

They gathered little rocks and lined them up on the railing of the deck. They scouted for baby pinecones and made patterns between the slats. The younger sat on the elder's lap talking about the pine trees and looking up at the sky to see the eagles and other birds flying close by. They got hot at the same time and drank ice water together and giggled, all the while wetting my eyes with tears of joy and gratitude to be a witness to this sight.

As of the writing of this memoir devotional of mine, they are eight and one hundred! They still love each other's company, eating French toast in the morning, playing board games after school, and going out for ice cream cones, seeing who will finish first! I couldn't ask for more. I'm the lucky chauffeur and get to come along for the ride! And what a ride it is.

I even get to share an ice cream too! :)

← PRICELESS PHOTO. THE VALUE OF A MOMENT ISN'T RECOGNIZED UNTIL IT'S A MEMORY. SAME GOES FOR A PHOTOGRAPH!

Time in the Truth

- **Psalm 100**
- **Psalm 133:1**
- **Proverbs 16:31**

Mirror Moment

A whole lot can be learned from this writing today. Maybe you've already chosen what you'll take away from it. What I glean is that wherever we find ourselves, likely sandwiched between the ages of eight and one hundred!, we value each minute and each encounter with the ones we love. Make memories, collect pinecones, and eat ice cream cones!

Communion with my Creator

Oh Father of us all, young and old,

Thank You. Thank You for the opportunity to see a young child who is newly discovering life around him and one who has lived almost all his years, who takes delight in those simple pleasures. May I learn from both of these dear ones in my "middle years," those undeniably busy, trying to stay ahead of the game and beat the odds kind of years. Bring me to the place of both new discovery and wise experience so that my today will be a combination of awestruck wonder and immense gratitude.

In Jesus' name! Amen

Song Suggestions

Song Title	Artist
The Blessing	Cody Carnes and Kari Jobe

Theme

Time Well Spent

Discussion Questions following *Love Across the Decades*

1. How has time dictated your life? Where has it been eaten up? Share a time when you felt you didn't use time wisely. How has growing older changed your idea and response to time?

2. Read **Psalm 100**. Make a list of all the verbs in **verses 1-4**. What or who is the object that should be receiving these actions? Now, personalize each sentence by writing your own sentences using each of these verbs (i.e., "**Shout** freely about God's goodness and faithfulness"). Share a line or two of your personal declarations about the Lord.

   When we truly live these declarations, how does this affect our interactions with others? Where can we do better?

3. How does **verse 5 of Psalm 100** speak to the devotion we read today? In thinking of the world and how we live today, what sadly challenges this generational richness?

4. Read **Psalm 133:1** in several translations... What words are used to describe how we are to live together? Are there areas of your life where doing this is hard/impossible? What can we do if this is true?

5. Read **Proverbs 16:31**. Most likely, those of us reading this devotional fall into the category of "gray hair"... How does Scripture say we attain this crown of splendor, and what can we commit to doing that will assure being found righteous?

6. Define "legacy" in your own words. How do you want to be remembered, and what are you doing to make sure that happens?

7. Make a mental note of who can benefit from your "gray hair" and live the truth, so generations of your family will know the love of Jesus.

8. Close by listening to the lyric-rich song suggestion and make it your prayer.

38. Hues

I don't know about you, but I love colors! All colors! Having our eyes opened wide to all the beautiful colors God created enriches our lives. I see varying hues as an expression of God's character and his desire to bring us pleasure. If we stop to appreciate them all, what a feast for our eyes and an expansion of our world!

When I look out over our deck, I see green... But I can't stop there; I see hunter green, pine tree green, blue spruce, jade, olive, spring, teal, turquoise, shamrock, forest, and sea green! Even if you aren't in the mountains to see the different shades, I bet you can look outside at the trees on your street and identify many hues as well. Hues are not confined to a mountain view!

Identifying shades of colors in the visual world is only the beginning of appreciating and understanding the beauty of colors—those we see with our eyes, as well as experience in our souls. Let's take a minute to identify how we often use hues to describe our feelings and how, if we do, it can help us to dissect and examine what might be happening within ourselves.

In general, and in my opinion, blue shades are often used to describe sadness. Reds, anger. Greens, envy. Yellows, happiness. But if we dig a little deeper and use a variety of shade words, like baby blue, azure, navy, sapphire, midnight, and so on, or crimson, scarlet, coral, and ruby, we may begin to better identify our feelings in a way we haven't before. I believe God gave us varieties of hues in order to bring richness to the seeing eye, as well as to the deep interweaving of our innermost being.

I don't mean to get all "far out" from reality, but since God Himself was the creator of colors, why not use them to identify hard emotions, embracing and sitting in them for a bit? And then, by adding gentler and more pleasing colors to soften the bitter, harsh tones, bringing us back to a more peaceful space?

For example, if I am sad and I say I feel like midnight blue, then if I add some white or a lighter shade of blue, or even gray tones, the midnight softens, and I'm able to see the world around me in a

← PRETTY AWESOME PHOTO IF I SAY SO MYSELF. AND YES, I TOOK IT, BUT DON'T CLAIM TO BE A PROFESSIONAL.

more pleasing light. Or by examining why we feel bright red anger, as long as we identify what brought us there, we can learn to deal positively with those severe feelings.

There is nothing wrong with feeling "midnight blue" or "bright red," as examples, for a while because of circumstances that brought you there. But also must eventually recognize what can be added in order to relieve the stress of the severity of the emotions.

In conclusion today, I believe using colors to identify what we are feeling and our mood may actually be incredibly helpful in understanding our own emotions AND expressing to others how we feel.

Time in the Truth

- **Ecclesiastes 3:1; 4-6**
- **Matthew 5:4; 9:36; 27:3**
- **John 11:35**
- **1 Corinthians 13:13**
- **Philippians 4:6, 7**
- **1 Thessalonians 5:18**

- **Psalm 16:11; 25:16; 27:3; 37:4; 42:11; 94:19**
- **Luke 22:44**
- **Romans 10:11; 12:15**
- **James 3:16**
- **Ephesians 4:26**
- **Hebrews 4:16**

Mirror Moment

As we personally examine our emotions and perhaps use colors to enhance the discovery of where we find ourselves emotionally, let's not forget that God uses all the colors—what we are feeling today and what we felt yesterday and may face tomorrow—to weave our tapestry. This exercise isn't to totally change the original color(s). It's an exercise in deepening the understanding of where we are emotionally and how God intends to use whatever we are feeling to draw us closer to Him and to appreciate the brilliance of all the hues.

Communion with my Creator

Today, I offer this poem as our prayer, beautifully written by Corrie ten Boom, survivor of the Holocaust and prolific writer and speaker.

"Life is But a Weaving"
My life is but a weaving between my God and me.
I cannot choose the colors, He weaveth steadily.
Oft times He weaveth sorrow, and I in foolish pride, forget He sees the upper, and I the underside.
Not 'til the loom is silent, and the shuttles cease to fly, will God unroll the canvas, and reveal the reason why.
The dark threads are as needful, in the weaver's skillful hand, as the threads of gold and silver, in the pattern He has planned.
He knows, He loves, He cares.
Nothing this truth can dim.
He gives the very best to those who leave the choice to Him.

Amen

Song Suggestion

Song Title	Artist
Your Grace Finds Me	Matt Redman

Theme

Depth of Emotions, Embracing all Emotions,

Perspective Change

Discussion Questions following *Hues*

1. In the 1970s there were mood rings you could buy that would change colors depending on your mood! If you had the "privilege" of remembering them, did you own one? What are your thoughts?

2. Where have you seen brilliant colors that have tantalized your eyes? Do you have a favorite color? And if so, why is it your favorite? What color describes the emotion you are feeling presently?

3. Share in reading the **verses** listed under the **Time In the Truth** section discussing the emotions presented in each one. If time allows, assign a creative color to each one :). You may also choose to pair up or get in smaller groups for this activity.

4. Discuss the pros and cons of each emotion found in the Scriptures, or any other emotions your group would like to discuss. Are some emotions always bad and others always good, or can all emotions find a place of value in our world?

5. How do you view the idea of adding in a bit of another color to change a shade you are feeling, whether it's to soften the turmoil of a situation or help you shift your perspective?

6. What color would you assign to gratitude and grace, and why? How do gratitude and grace add to our emotional well-being, and what happens to other emotions when gratitude and grace are added in?

7. End your time today by reading Corrie ten Boom's poem and listening to "Your Grace Finds Me" by Matt Redman.

39. Pine Trees

What is your favorite scent? We've talked about favorite sights, sounds, and colors, so why not our favorite smells! Aromas can evoke memories, stir up our taste buds, and even bring us serenity. I know that some smells can also bring up negative past experiences, as all of our senses can do. We'll touch upon all of these as we unpack how important fragrance is to our Creator!

Olfaction is the sense of smell. Our ability to smell wakes up other senses too! In the mountains, the forest of pine trees has a distinct aroma. That aroma, in scientific studies, has the ability to actually bring about a calming effect, lowering stress and anxiety levels, which in turn reduces blood pressure and heart rate! The blessing of this fragrance is not only physical but emotional as well, bringing about relaxation and peace.

Now, how does all this relate to our lives, other than right about now we all wish we could be breathing in that fresh mountain air, mingled with scents of pine, earth, wildflowers, and wood! ;) Fragrances and aromas are actually mentioned several places in Scripture, describing how priests would offer up burnt offerings as a soothing aroma to the Lord. We are still being asked to do the same with our very lives today!

As much as I enjoy and reap the benefits of the smell of pine trees and fresh mountain air, I also find pleasing the bouquet coming from loved ones and friends who simply have a presence about them that accomplishes that very same thing, and more! Ones that provide me direction, accountability, stability, peace, and calm, ever pointing me to Jesus and His Word.

Scripture describes how we are to be a fragrance of Christ in all our interactions with others. Take time now to examine yourself and the "scent you put off" when you walk into a crowded room, a business meeting, or a hospital room. When you have conversations with your spouse, or as you walk down the crowded aisles of a grocery store, your very presence speaks loudly. Your "scent" is either a pleasing fragrance or a bad odor.

Whiff, whiff, which shall it be?

Time in the Truth

- **John 12:1-7**
- **Ephesians 5:1, 2; 3-21**
- **2 Corinthians 2:14-17**

Mirror Moment

Who will I cross paths with today that could benefit from the aroma of Christ? Does my witness look like Jesus, or does it reek of the world? Remind me that everywhere I go there is an opportunity to either stand out and show Jesus or to add to the stench of the culture around me.

Communion with my Creator

Dear Creator of All Good Gifts,

What a gift You gave us when You created our sense of smell. If I am ever anything other than a pleasing aroma to You, my Lord, make me aware of the changes in my life that I need to make. Humble me and make my life reflect Your fragrance wherever I go.

In Jesus' name! Amen

Song Suggestions

Song Title	Artist
Perfume	Bryan and Katie Torwalt
The Fragrance	Eileen and Tommy Walker

Theme

Having the Fragrance of Christ

Discussion Questions following *Pine Trees*

1. Name some favorite smells or scents, and share why they are pleasant to you!

2. The books of Leviticus and Numbers are filled with sacrifices and offerings that were required to be brought before God in order to atone for their sins and to be in right standing with God. These offerings and sacrifices are often declared to be a "pleasing and soothing aroma to the Lord." Why do you think God expresses it this way and uses this metaphor?

3. **John 12:1-7** is a portion of the story of Mary pouring perfume on Jesus' feet. Why do you think she did this? What powerful lesson is being shown to everyone in that room, and even to us today? How does the latter half of this verse remind us of what happens when a sweet smell fills the air?

4. In the New Testament we know Jesus' sacrifice replaced the need for constant offerings and sacrifices, which had been necessary in the Old Testament. Once we recognize the importance of aroma in the Old Testament, we can more easily understand why Scripture describes even our lives as being a pleasing aroma when we follow in Jesus' footsteps. With this in mind, discuss how our aroma is pleasing to God in how we act, react, and relate to others in our lives.

5. A beautiful picture of how we are to live is found in **Ephesians 5:1, 2,** and again, the importance of *Jesus' sacrifice!* Continue to read **Ephesians 5:3-21** and discover what the opposite of a pleasing aroma looks like in our lives. Which of these things listed are still real temptations for you? Or have been in the past?

6. Reading **2 Corinthians 2:14-17** (read in the MSG version as well) further impresses on us how our aroma of Christ is a symbol of both death and life. Discuss how both of these are true.

7. In closing today's discussion, pray and listen to one or both of the songs listed in the song suggestions. They are both beautiful expressions of how our lives are pleasing aromas to Him.

40. Glow-in-the-Dark Stars

My children had glow-in-the-dark stars on their walls and ceilings when they were young, and my grands have them on theirs now. It is a nice touch to their bedrooms when they are going to sleep and the lights go out to see the lit-up "stars" giving some luminescence to the room. They can bring some comfort to a dark room and help the littles go to sleep.

However, NOTHING compares to the real thing—the hundreds of stars in the night sky, easily seen on clear nights in the mountains where there isn't the distraction of light pollution from other sources. I know we've already discussed stars, but I'd like to do a little bit of comparison and find a truth hidden within them. Glow-in-the-dark stars parallel the night sky stars. This comparison easily teaches us the difference between what appears real and what is truly real.

We can all agree that glow-in-the-dark stars are temporary. They rely on lamps and overhead lights to bring them what little illumination they give off before they go dark. At first glance, they look comforting, but they fade quickly, hopefully not before the youngsters are fast asleep. The lights in the night sky, on the other hand, are each illuminated with their own brilliant light, far surpassing the cheap imitation.

How often do we settle for a substitute in our lives instead of choosing what is best and authentic? We find temporary pleasures, or habits that dull the discomfort, or put off dealing with our "stuff," only to find there is no satisfaction or true joy in the fleeting, momentary distraction. We cut corners, settle for less, choose stuff over substance, believe lies instead of searching for the truth, and wallow in our hurts rather than seek true healing.

Glow-in-the-dark stars are fine for children's bedrooms. But we must go beyond the four walls of a bedroom to discover the incredible light that comes from the real thing. Don't settle for anything less than authentic for yourself, your relationship with God, and with others.

Time in the Truth

- **Ecclesiastes 2:1-11**
- **Isaiah 40**

Mirror Moment

Have you ever found a temporary solution to be better than a permanent one?

Whether it be eating to satisfy a craving that has nothing to do with your true hunger, or taking a drug to dull the pain of a reality you find yourself in, or seeking approval from any sources other than the Source of grace and truth Himself...

Scan your memory for a time when you settled instead of searching for the best, most long-lasting, eternal solution. When it comes to our lives, ONLY the best should do! Partnering with the Maker of the Stars can light up your darkness and bring lasting satisfaction.

Communion with my Creator

Dear True Satisfier,

Shine the light on the areas in my life where I am settling for less than Your best for me. Give me the courage to face and uproot the temporary solutions and short-term pleasures and return to Your truth and restoration. I only choose You!

In Jesus' name! Amen

Song Suggestion

Song Title	Artist
Holy Forever	CeCe Winans

Theme

Temporary Pleasures, Don't Settle for Less

than God's Grace AND Truth!

Discussion Questions following *Glow-in-the-Dark Stars*

1. Why do we sometimes settle for less than the best, or the authentic, in our lives?

2. Take time to ask yourself the question posed in the Mirror Moment—"Have you ever found temporary solutions to be better than a permanent one?"

3. Read **Ecclesiastes 2:1-11**. What lessons can we learn from this set of verses?

4. Can you think of a time in Scripture (and there are many) when a temporary solution was chosen over the best solution? Where someone relied on their own knowledge, power, or strength. *For help in answering, check out the ideas below the questions.

5. The sentence from the devotional that reads, "We cut corners, settle for less, choose stuff over substance, believe lies instead of searching for the truth, wallow in our pain rather than seek true healing..." is packed with many temporary "fixes." Which one of these has been a temptation or a reality for you? How has that turned out for the situation and for your heart?

6. On the flip side, can you think of times in Scripture where someone relied on the Power and Strength of God when faced with choices, instead of temporary ones? How did these choices, even against all odds, prove to be the best option? How did God show up, and how was He glorified? *For help, check below.

7. When in YOUR life has God shown up when you chose the best over the easy or temporary? If you have trouble answering this question, read and answer the last two questions.

8. **Isaiah 40** speaks of the Mighty Power of God. Read it aloud with your group and let the truth of choosing ONLY the genuine, authentic Power of God be your guiding force as you face choices each day. Will you choose "the glow-in-the-dark stars OR the real thing?!"

9. Listen to "Holy Forever" and be reminded that He is greater than anything we face in life. He is able to make the temptations dissipate, and settling for anything less is no longer appealing. He is Holy and beyond Big, making settling no longer an option!!

    a. Look up the lyrics to this powerful song and claim them as your own!

    b. If time allows, look up verses on the Holiness of God!

    *A few Biblical characters to help in answering the questions:

    4. Adam and Eve, Saul, many Kings of Israel, David (Bathsheba and Uriah); Solomon (last part of his reign), Jonah, Judas, Saul before becoming Paul

    6. Ruth, Rahab, Shadrach..., Daniel, Peter, and John (after the resurrection), Paul (after he was Saul)

41. When (We Think) No One Is Watching

A few years back, a car drove by our cabin and stopped at the bend in the road by a sign that reads "Granny June," which, by the way, has been there for years, and no one quite knows who Granny June is or was. :) I was somewhat out of sight on our deck and behind some trees. I wasn't trying to be nosy; it's just that the road was very visible from my vantage point. Without warning, the couple in the car got out. I could tell they really weren't familiar with the area since they seemed a little lost looking around. I was about to call to them and ask if they needed help, hoping I didn't startle them. But before I could, they startled me, BIG time. One of them pulled their pants down and began to use the forest floor as their bathroom. It's not like they even moved off the road, found a tree to squat behind, or even went around their car... It was a sight I had never seen before, haven't seen since, and hope to never see again!! And it was not the male of the couple either... if you needed a further understanding of the visual I witnessed.

But it got me thinking about how often "we think" no one is watching, and we do things we probably aren't proud of or should think twice about doing or saying in the first place. I know in my life there have been times I've wrestled, especially with feelings I shouldn't be having or attitudes I am not proud of. If I were truly transparent, some who think the best of me might not think so highly of me. I'm ashamed of those feelings and attitudes, honestly. When I sit and consider this however, I realize we all probably find ourselves in this position at some time in our lives. Not the scenario I mentioned at first, but the one where we have done, said, or thought things we are less than proud of. So, if we are truly honest with ourselves about this, let's tackle this issue head-on. It's what we do with those thoughts, attitudes, actions, and words that can either bring healing, freedom, and righteous behavior or keep us hiding in the place of guilt and shame.

There is a word that may be confusing to us but speaks well to how this healing and freedom can be achieved. The word is "repent."

It's simply recognizing and admitting where we've been wrong, feeling sorry and remorseful for doing it, laying it down, then leaving it at the foot of the cross, and literally turning the other way. The process of making things right usually consists of confessing and/or apologizing where needed and then filling our minds with all things good and right, with the help of the Holy Spirit and Scripture to make all things new. We don't have to live a life of lies or deceit, shame, and guilt for our actions and reactions. Jesus doesn't want us to stay there. He provides a way to true peace, through repentance and forgiveness. And then allow Him to be our righteousness. I have definitely touched on some of these concepts in previous devotionals, but I feel the lesson on integrity is one we can never get enough of as human beings.

Now, I'm not sure the couple in the car on the bend of the road ever saw me. I turned away quickly and went inside. But if they did, I won't hold that against them, just like a sincere apology and genuine attitude of repentance will heal the hurts and wounds of the heart kind.

Time in the Truth

- Isaiah 29:15, 16
- Psalm 32
- Psalm 51
- John 3:16
- Romans 8:1-11
- 1 John 1:9
- 2 Corinthians 10:3-7
- Philippians 4:6-9

Mirror Moment

Are you the same when no one is looking as you are when you are in the spotlight? Have you been caught with "your pants down"? Being true and open with yourself is the only way you can and will come to the point of repentance that leads to freedom and righteousness. Hidden sin is where Satan wants you to live. Don't fall for it, or stay stuck there. Forgiveness is one of the greatest gifts God has offered us in this life. Take advantage of His love and gift of mercy and grace, and pass it along. Tell someone today about your decision to repent (in the truest sense of that word) and be free. And find an accountability partner.

Communion with my Creator

Merciful and Forgiving God,

How unworthy I am. Yet You love me. I recognize my need for You. You are El Roi, the God who sees. This fact both exhilarates me and frightens me. You see me at my best, and You see me at my worst. The sacrifice of Your Only Son for our salvation provided the Way, the Truth, and the Life. Reveal in me where I need to repent and ask for forgiveness. I know confession is the only way to repentance. May I live my life with the words of David on my tongue, "The sacrifices of God are a broken spirit, a broken and contrite heart, God, You will not despise."

In Jesus' name! Amen

Song Suggestions

Song Title	Artist
Create In Me a Clean Heart	Keith Green
Here's My Heart Lord	Casting Crowns
O Come to the Altar	Elevation Worship

Theme
Repentance, Integrity, Being Authentic and Genuine

Discussion Questions following *When (We Think) No One Is Watching*

1. Have you ever seen something you'd like to unsee but can't? Could this become a jumping-off place to learn a lesson or be taught a truth you otherwise didn't know you needed to learn?

2. Read **Isaiah 29:15, 16**. Why is thinking God doesn't see or know what we have done in secret so arrogant? What do you have buried inside that should come out from hiding? Why have you hidden it? Share openly if you can. However, if you can't, I challenge you to face those deep,

hidden places or behaviors wholeheartedly, whether you share out loud or not. Doing so will help you experience the real peace I reference in the devotional. Then authentic integrity has a place to flourish. The Scriptures we read today will hopefully give you a road map to that place! Pause before moving forward in this study, and pray for whatever you may be holding onto in secret. You may choose to listen to one of the song suggestions now, and one as you close today.

3. Psalm 32's subtitle is "Blessedness of Forgiveness and of Trust in God." As you read **Psalm 32**, stop to make a list of the results of hiding your wrongdoings. Then another list of the advantages that come from transparency and trust in God. You have to admit, they are the furthest of opposites! What steps are mentioned in this passage that allow the release of pent-up feelings, attitudes, and behaviors we aren't proud of, which lead to the benefits of blessings?

4. **Psalm 51** takes our study to an even deeper level. I ask you to consider personalizing it as well. This Psalm was written by David, after Nathan the prophet came to him, and David finally confessed his adultery with Bathsheba and the horrible outcome of his attempted cover-up. (If you are unfamiliar with this story of David, it can be found in **2 Samuel 11**.) Consider each of these questions, and while doing so, place your own hidden, secretive sin foremost in your mind.

    a. What does David confess? What do you need to confess?

    b. What does David ask of God? What are you asking of God?

    c. What does David say God is capable of? What do you know God is capable of?

    d. How will David use what he has learned from these grave sins? How will you use what you have learned from your separation?

    e. What does David realize God actually wants from his children? What does God want from you?

5. Return to the paragraph in the devotional that introduces and defines the word "repent." If you haven't already discussed this word and its meaning, do so now, and apply this to an example of what might be "a hidden sin." What is required when repentance is real? Read **John 3:16, Romans 8:1-11**, and **1 John 1:9** to understand how and why repentance is possible!

6. Read **2 Corinthians 10:3-7** paying close attention to verses **5 through 7**. What depth can these verses add to your discussion on living with integrity? Note: Paul was writing to the church in Corinth defending his own integrity. Consider reading this set of verses in the MSG version!

7. **Philippians 4:6-9** helps complete the map we have been plotting out for ourselves in order to arrive at the place of highest integrity. What are we told to think on in verse 8 that replaces the once hidden thoughts? After you read this passage, discuss some specifics of how to do this.

8. Close with the communion prayer and another one of the song suggestions.

42. Seasons

Change. What does this word conjure up in your mind? Does it excite you or make you cringe? I do believe it isn't an easy word for many of us. Change means shifting, modifying, and altering. Change often brings an awkward, uncomfortable feeling. Uncharted territory and unknown tomorrows. But before I continue with the idea that change is a doomsday topic or something to fear, let me remind you of why change is so important, as well as inevitable.

God designed us to change. He doesn't ever want us to remain stagnant. Stagnation causes a lack of growth and development. God never intended us to remain in that space. He wants us to grow and make room for new and different things, as hard as it is sometimes.

This is beautifully illustrated in the change of seasons and how God's entire creation depends on the cycle of change, from the new life of flowers and trees in spring to the change of colors in the fall and the impending end, ushering in cold and frost. I see this so pronounced in the colors of the aspen trees, the freezing morning temperatures in early fall, and the budding of new life in the springtime up at the cabin. Certainly, the changes of the seasons can be seen everywhere, not just in the mountains, and therefore, are familiar to all.

Transitioning into a discussion about our lives, sometimes change comes by our own hand, sometimes we are suddenly thrust into a whirlwind of change beyond our control, and other changes creep slowly and dauntingly into our normal. Whatever way change arrives, *how we face it is the key to how change will affect us*. We can either flourish in our new space by adjusting and embracing it or crumble, choosing to attempt to hold onto how things used to be. I'm not implying this is easy, only that it is necessary if we desire to find joy in every stage of this thing we call life.

The Earth's cycle of seasons reflect our lives in such a stunning way! There is beauty in each season, and we should embrace each one of them. I believe one reason God gave us the change of seasons was for us to recognize the comparison to our lives, expecting the changes and choosing to find loveliness in every single one.

← MY HUSBAND ENJOYING AN EARLY FALL DAY SITTING BY
   A NEIGHBOR'S STREAM AND ASPEN.

Time in the Truth

- **Hebrews 13:5-8**

In the following 2 sets of verses, consider the changes the Israelites were experiencing and all they'd experienced. Then find the command of God, the promise of God, and the response of the people.
- **Joshua 1:1-13**
- **Isaiah 40; 41:10; 58:6-14; Lamentations 3:19-26**

In the next set of verses, discover all the amazing promises of God beautifully expressed.

- **Psalm 23; 121; 139**
- **Psalm 27; 46; 91**
- **Psalm 51; 103**
- **Psalm 100; 145**
- **2 Corinthians 12:9**
- **Romans 8:28**
- **Philippians 4:19**
- **1 Peter 5:7**
- **John 14:3**
- **Revelation 21:4**

Mirror Moment

The simple definition of "change" is "to make different, alter, or modify." This fact can be scary, but it can also stir up hope and expectation, depending on how we view change. Spend a few minutes considering how you view change. How can the verses about hope and His promises in the Time in the Truth section help you to view change with anticipation instead of dread?

Communion with my Creator

Dear God of the Seasons and of Change,

Just as You are the God of the Seasons in nature, You are also the God of the Seasons of our lives. From our birth on this Earth to our Eternity, You created us for change. Where I am fearful of change, bring me to the place of acceptance. Where I am scared of what might come, provide comfort. Where the unknown brings anxiety, I ask You for the peace that passes human understanding. And remind me of Your goodness and Your faithfulness throughout all generations.

Thank You for being the God who NEVER changes. You are the ONE constant in our lives that makes change, new seasons, and a new "normal" not just bearable but embraceable. Praise God from whom all blessings flow!

In Jesus' name! Amen

Song Suggestions

Song Title	Artist
It is Well With My Soul	Audrey Assad
Every Season	Nichole Nordeman

Theme

Appreciating and Accepting Each Season of Life,

Change, God's Promises

Discussion Questions following *Seasons*

1. Does change excite or scare you? Why?

2. Do you believe the statement, "How we face change is the key to how change will affect us"? How could expecting change impact us? Both negatively and positively.

3. God's Promises! Today we'll spend time reading, meditating on, and embracing God's promises beginning with **Hebrews 13:5-8**, because there is ONLY ONE who doesn't ever change! How does this Truth solidify our foundation?

4. As you begin to deep dive into Scripture today, use the guidance given in the "Time in the Truth" section and the verses listed to direct your discussion.

   You may also want to use the following questions as you unpack the promises in the verses that our Heavenly Father has given to us all!

   a. What words jump off the page to you?

   b. What comfort do they bring?

   c. What conviction do they pose?

   d. How should we respond when we embrace them?

   e. How do they affect our relationships?

   f. If you don't mind writing in your Bible, consider highlighting each of these promises, maybe even writing them down in a journal or notebook to read at a moment's notice. Personally, I like sticky notes, so I can see them all over my mirror!

   You may choose to do the questions above as a group or break up into smaller groups in order to get more input from everyone. After you've read the verses in pairs or individually, come back together and share what the Lord has shown you as you've read them.

   Change is inevitable, yet God never does!

5. Both of the song suggestions are well worth the listen. Don't forget to close with prayer.

43. Four Small Hikes

I take the pup on at least four, sometimes six or eight, small walks up, around, and behind our cabin daily when we're on the mountain. She enjoys the sniffs and can do her "business" each time! I enjoy the exercise and the scenery. I see something new every time if I just look around!

Sometimes we set out on a longer hike, up or down and around the mountain. However, I realize those four or more smaller doses amount to the same distance and provide my pup and me the necessary breaks to refuel and enjoy them more. Each small hike amounts to 1/3 of a mile, so I am getting decent exercise by the end of the day, and our pooch is happy too!

I am also a goal setter! I always have been. Maybe you are too! However, as I've grown older, I have learned to take my time in reaching my goals. Giving myself grace when I stumble, learning from each step, and taking my time enjoying the journey, as I work toward my desired objective. You see, when I was younger, I saw the end result as the only win. The thing that should be attained in one big jump, or in one day, pressuring myself to be the best of whatever it was I was doing! I wish I had my older self to tell my younger self that the stages from beginning to end could be more fully satisfying if I could enjoy the stages leading to the goal. And also, along the journey, there are many surprising benefits, most of which are lost or never discovered if I am just rushing to the finish line. I know I've touched on this concept several times in earlier lessons, but I believe Jesus would want us to learn this lesson from how He lived his life on Earth. So that's where we'll spend our time today. Learning to live our lives reflecting His example. He lived slowly and purposefully. He lived connecting with anyone and everyone who crossed his path. I intend to finish my days with this in mind, trying not to get ahead of the process.

Whether I take five short walks or one long hike for the day, I will set out with the perspective of noticing my surroundings, smelling the pine trees along the way, stopping to talk to neighbors, and asking God to make me walk in His steps and with His purpose.

Time in the Truth

- **Psalm 127:1, 2**
- **Mark 1:35; 6:46**
- **Luke 5:16**
- **Luke 10:38-42**
- **Luke 2:42-52; 19:1-10**

- **John 4:1-30**
- **Matthew 15:29-39**
- **Psalm 90:12-17**
- **Ephesians 5:15-21**

Mirror Moment

"Stop and smell the..." "Wake up and smell the..." Take time to smell the..." We've all heard these idioms ending with "roses," which signify a beautiful journey. But have you ever truly lived by them? Or have you been so busy, like me, that you consider the goal as the only win? To make the most of every minute along your way today, ask God for new lenses to see what He has for every encounter and every "chance" meeting and enrich you and everyone around you. The endgame isn't the only win!

Communion with my Creator

Dear Heavenly Pace-Maker,

Keep me in step with You. Slow and purposeful, not rushed and missing the journey You've carved out for me to live. Show me what that looks like in my life as I go about my days, in order to bring You glory and honor.

In Jesus' name! Amen

Song Suggestions

Song Title	Artist
Be Thou My Vision	Audrey Assad
Worn	Tenth Avenue North

Theme

One Step at a Time, Joy in the Journey

Discussion Questions following *Four Small Hikes*

1. Are you a goal setter? If so, has it served you well? If you are not, has that served you well? Is it hard for you to slow down? What screams at you to keep the frantic pace? How does control play a role in how you view using time? How does **Psalm 127:1, 2** begin to help us unpack our use of time? Listen to the song suggestion, "Worn," before you begin the rest of the study. While listening, consider if weariness and heaviness play a part in your definition of time and reaching your goals.

2. Was Jesus a goal setter? What do you think His view of time was and still is? Are goal setting and pacing our time, compatible? How can we embrace both?

3. Today, we are going to spend our study together in the Gospels, focusing on how Jesus used time during his stay on Earth and what we can learn from it. Begin by reading **Mark 1:35, 6:46**, and **Luke 5:16** and recognize where Jesus got His guidance. How has this practice been helpful to you? When you haven't, how has this affected your use of time?

4. How do you view time? Is it a scarce commodity, a linear version, using words such as "wasting," "spending," "budgeting," and "saving" time? Attaching time to a clock and a calendar. OR, do you see time as cyclical, with an unlimited supply of it, spending more time learning from the past, reflecting and growing from past time, and eager about the present and future time?

    There is value to time. As U.S. Americans and other "cold-natured" countries who favor the first line of thinking, we could learn a thing or two from our Earth's "warm-natured" countries, who usually embrace the second-line definition of time. Most importantly, what type of time did Jesus live?

5. **Luke 10:38-42** gives a good illustration of Jesus' view of time. How does this differ from how we use time?

6. Discover for yourselves some of the lessons Jesus taught to unlikely characters, the parables He used, and the miracles He performed. How can we learn from His pace of life? Some examples, and a very short list, include:

   Luke 2:42-52
   Luke 19:1-10
   John 4:1-30
   Matthew 15:29-39

   There are many Scriptures here. Pick and choose what will be the most meaningful for your group, or choose your own stories from Jesus' life to discuss.

7. Make sure you save part of your group's gathering to discuss the following passages. They warn us about using our time wisely, why this is important, and how to balance it now that we have a better understanding of it. Read **Psalm 90:12-17** and **Ephesians 5:15-21**.

8. Close by listening to "Be Thou My Vision" as your prayer.

44. Unfinished Business

I've told you all about the amazing beauty of our little piece of Heaven. I've doted on almost every inch of our little mountain experience. I hope you've been able to almost "taste and see" this place, even if you've never had the pleasure of visiting.

However, there is a scene that is so unlike the rest of the mountain, and I would be remiss to leave this message out. The plot of land is a horrible eyesore, not too far from our cabin, up and around the bend. We can't see it from our place, but it is visible when we climb up the mountain on our walks, not too far away. It is a glaring and ugly sight when anyone passes by. It sticks out like some ghoul among the beauty of everything else around.

Evidently, years ago, someone had the idea of building a place; they must have bought the property, spent some time and money to haul in "tons" of cinderblocks, and began to build in the hopes of producing something wonderful. Then, they stopped. That's right, they just stopped. Did the money run out? Did the person no longer have any interest? Was there dissension in the family, or worse? I don't know. But what I do know is that everyone would agree it is an unattractive sight to see among the beauty surrounding it. The project has become an eyesore, a stark difference from everything else on our mountain.

I've considered working this blot on the landscape into my writings in the past, but the time wasn't right, and neither was the message. However, just the other day as I walked past it, the message was loud and clear, mainly because this time, when I laid eyes on it, this messy spot seemed personal. I could relate to the feeling of its sadness and pain. "Unfinished business" of the resentful kind can and usually does become messy and ugly. And maybe once I explain, you can relate as well. Recently, I discovered I had something unresolved in my heart and head. It was a regret I wish I didn't have to own up to, and even though it wasn't all my fault or anyone else's, more the condition of a situation, for purposes of healing, I knew I needed to work on mending and restoration. The regret, also known as my *fruitless longing*, led me to bitterness, also known as unforgiveness, that had *fermented*. Which, in turn, hindered and altered some very dear and close relationships. The longer I held onto the sadness, which turned foul, the more I lived in the cycle of pain, which led to anger and blame and unresolved conflict with people I loved. Living in that kind of ache isn't living at all. It's surviving and pretending, and that is no way to live.

What became clear once I finally got sick and tired of being stuck in my own head was the gift that could lead to freedom and restoration. The gift was that of admission, confession, surrender, and forgiveness. They are gifts worth opening and embracing. Hard as it was to have to own up to and admit my part in the sadness, it is what has brought peace back into my soul. It can for you as well. Not much new revelation has happened in the situation besides time, but I rest in knowing I am not chained to the fruitless longing and unsettledness that plagued my actions, reactions, and interactions during that season of my life.

I must close this writing with the fact that the eyesore on the landscape is still there and doesn't appear to be remedied anytime soon. It will stand as a reminder to me of how I could still be living that messiness inside, but with Jesus guiding my decision, I chose and still choose to this day surrender, freedom, acceptance, and peace in its place.

Time in the Truth

- **Hebrews 12:1, 2**
- **James 3:16**
- **1 Peter 5:6, 7**
- **Galatians 5:13-18; 6:1**
- **Ephesians 4:30-32**
- **Galatians 6:1**
- **Matthew 16:27**
- **Acts 20:24**
- **Psalm 139:23, 24**
- **Philippians 3:12-14**

Mirror Moment

Use the next few minutes to consider asking Jesus to help you uncover any "unfinished business" that has resulted in discontentment, bitterness, anger, regret, or grief in your life, showing up in actions and reactions you are not proud of. Or maybe you are just "stuck in your head" with the pain or a stain you don't want to live with anymore!

Consider what it would take to admit, confess, and surrender the control of it, asking for forgiveness and then forgiving yourself. Facing these giants will allow them to no longer have power over you! The results can be so freeing and bring peace over your "tired and weary." Only through searching yourself and prayer—you don't have to go it alone—can this truly come to pass. The process can be slow and painstaking, yet amazingly worth it.

Recently, as I was beginning to uncover my own "unfinished business," I read this quote, which actually stabbed me right between my eyes and prompted me to seek healing. It is so worth sharing with you: "Like good fruit, the fruit of bitterness will also reproduce after itself. It is a natural occurrence, just like weeds in a garden. Left unchecked, the weeds in your life will become your life, and since weeds are good for nothing, your life will become the same." —Author unknown.

Please don't let this happen.

Communion with my Creator

Dear Regret Eraser,

I come contrite and broken. I recognize where I have been a part of my own unfinished business. The space is messy... (Finish your own prayer. I have.)

In Jesus' name! Amen

Song Suggestion

Song Title	Artist
Rebel Heart	Lauren Daigle

Theme

Bitterness, Resentment, Anger, Regret, Sadness, Finishing Well

Side Note: We have addressed the topics of conflict, repentance, surrendering, forgiveness, creating boundaries, and then healing and freedom in several different devotionals scattered throughout this book. So this may seem like a repeat. And in some ways, yes, it is. I've even considered removing one or more of those devotionals, thinking I've focused too much on these themes. But then I recall how God, over the course of writing Scripture, revisited many of these issues multiple times due to us as humans not learning the lesson the first time. If you feel it is too similar, by all means move on. However, if you have at least one area of life where you continue to feel stuck, or any form of regret in life, I ask that you hang in there for one more metaphor on these subjects. :) And ask God to reveal something new to you as you read and study.

Discussion Questions following *Unfinished Business*

1. Have you ever had a project you started and didn't finish? If so, why didn't you? Did you start out excited about it? What happened to make you quit?

2. Regret. Pick apart the next few questions one at a time. What is regret? When does it happen to us? How does this affect us and our relationships? Where can we go once we live there? Why do some choose to remain there? Is regret always a bad thing?

3. What does it mean to be "stuck in your head"? How do we get out of that mindset? How does the phrase "being stuck in your head" perpetuate regret? How can **Hebrews 12:1, 2** help with answering these questions?

4. Let's dive into Scripture that will hopefully bring new insights and conviction on how to recognize and deal with regret, being stuck in our heads, and finishing well:

a. **James 3:16**... How is jealousy a cousin to regret?

b. **1 Peter 5:6, 7**... Why do humility and regret vie for the same space in our heads?

c. **Galatians 5:13-18**... Find two key concepts that can't live alongside regret.

d. **Ephesians 4:30-32**... Who hurts even more than us when we harbor sin? What is the solution?

e. **Galatians 6:1**... How does looking into a mirror shed light on our part in a "sadness"? Why are we often reluctant to do this?

f. **Matthew 16:27**... How do these words of Jesus convict us to deal with the hurt we've caused?

g. **Acts 20:24**... What was Paul's truth, and should it be ours too?

h. **Psalm 139:23, 24**... Ask God to help you lay down the pride, the angst, the anger, and the bitterness that have led to the regret you've been harboring.

i. **Philippians 3:12-14**... Read this set of verses and ask God to help you finish well, whether that's finishing in a certain situation, a season, or in the rest of life here on Earth.

5. Whatever you do, give attention to your "unfinished business." Humble yourselves, whether it means restoring and finishing the eyesore or tearing it down and beginning again. But whatever it is, be willing, with the help of the Scripture and Holy Spirit, to do the work. Read again the quote in the last paragraph of the Mirror Moment. Let that motivate you to end well wherever there is regret.

6. Look up the opposite of regret... and you find that words like "satisfaction," "contentment," "fulfillment," "delight," and "joy" top the list!! Aim to live there, doing what it takes. What is stopping you?

7. Listen to the song suggestion and write your own/group prayer, adding everyone's input!

45. Judgment Call Part 1: Deer "Play"

I hate to admit what I'm about to write. I'll claim ignorance before we even get started.

As my husband and I were walking down the road not far from our cabin, we spotted a deer crossing the road. To our surprise, it didn't just gracefully prance on through the woods like they usually do. It stopped and stared. Then it turned, *as if* it wanted to make friends with us, and more importantly, with our puppy, who was playfully sniffing and running up ahead. The deer *seemed* to want to play, hopping about and staying close, but not too close. We quickly recorded what we could on our phones, which *appeared* to be two of God's creatures getting along in a playful manner. Lanie, our 2-year-old Labradoodle at the time, decided this wasn't a safe place and ran to the other side of the road.

Since the deer didn't leave, we encouraged her to go back over and "play" with the deer. We commented on how we'd never witnessed a scene like this: making up in our minds that this deer was somehow domesticated and wanted to have a cordial and playful time with our dog. Lanie finally complied, since she's a good dog that way, and ran over to the deer for a better look. Well, it was in that instant that the tiny spotted fawn sprang up nearby them both, and Mama Doe came for our dog.

As you can guess, our instincts and ignorant assumptions were clearly very WRONG.

We began to shout loudly as the deer pounced on Lanie, and she ran to us! The doe, thank goodness, turned away and followed her fawn deep into the woods nearby.

← ONE OF MANY OPPORTUNITIES TO CAPTURE A PHOTO OF ONE OF GOD'S AMAZING CREATURES..

Things are NOT always what they seem to be. Being aware, educated, and wise makes for a much clearer picture of the scene, both on the mountain road and in life. Trusting too quickly and giving more access to ourselves before understanding what others may want or desire from us can and will likely lead to being "attacked by the deer." Having sober-minded friends, unlike my husband and me in the deer scenario, seeking God's ideal for our relationships and situations in our lives, and taking time to survey the situation before jumping to conclusions are *always* the best ideas!

Time in the Truth

- Proverbs 2:1-13
- Psalm 119:66
- Hosea 14:9

- 1 Corinthians 2:14-16
- Romans 12:2
- Philippians 1:9-11

Mirror Moment

Rethinking how we assume or prejudge our circumstances, the world around us, and our relationships takes an examination of self. This *can* and *should* be a practice we all participate in, making certain our motives, character, and integrity are in line with what God desires for us as His children and the witness we should be to our world. Today, as you go about your daily routine, examine your intentions in your actions and your speech, asking the Father to reveal where you may need redirection and clarity.

Communion with my Creator

To the God Who Sees,

Remind me of how limited my vision is, yet how absolutely clear Yours is. Thank You for being the wisest One, so I don't have to always understand. I choose to trust You. Give me discernment in my dealings. Surround me with friends who will always point to You, even revealing areas where I need to take inventory of my motivations, actions, and reactions that are not in line with the truth. Humble me.

In Jesus' name! Amen

Song Suggestions

Song Title	Artist
Discerning of Spirits	Darren Winfield
The Perfect Wisdom of God	Keith and Kristyn Getty

Theme

Assumptions, Hasty Judgments, Discernment, Wisdom

Discussion Questions following *Judgment Call Part 1: Deer "Play"*

1. Do you know anyone with the gift of discernment? If so, have they ever shared how this spiritual gift has been a blessing, and maybe even a curse, at times?

2. How can knowledge help us when we are trying to discern a situation? What's the difference between knowledge and wisdom? What can wisdom add that knowledge can't?

3. **Proverbs 2:1-13**. Read verse 9 first and consider the first word... "then"... read **verses 1-9** together and discuss all the actions leading up to being able to discern what is good and right. Finally, read **verses 11-13** to see the benefits of being discerning.

4. After reading **Psalm 119:66** and **Hosea 14:9**, discuss what it means to be taught good discernment and to walk in it.

5. After reading **1 Corinthians 2:14-16**, discuss what it means to have spiritual discernment and to have the mind of Christ. Consider reading this set of verses and all of the remaining ones for this lesson in the Amplified Bible for a deeper and clearer understanding!

6. The message in **Romans 12:2** speaks to me on so many levels. How does this verse align and follow up with even more understanding of the verses read in the previous question? Define "conform" and "transform", and pay attention to the "so that..."in this verse.

7. Judging situations and judging people are totally different. What are the differences? We will discuss judging people in depth in our next devotional, so don't spend too much time on it here.

8. Re-read the mirror moment. How do our motives, character, and integrity play a large role in discernment?

9. After reading **Philippians 1:9-11**, what are the elements for finishing well?

10. As always, end your time by listening to one of the song suggestions and praying.

46. Judgment Call Part 2: First Impressions

For the second week in a row, I am not pleased with myself concerning the story I'm about to share with you. I could claim ignorance in the previous devotional, however this time I clearly made a judgment call that was unwarranted and was directed at a person and not a situation. I am not proud of myself. These are lessons we all need to learn, and if someone reading this can keep from making this mistake, it will have been worth being vulnerable to my readers.

I have the privilege of contacting ministers during the summer to come and preach a sermon and stay for a week in a small cabin next door to the outdoor chapel area in our mountain community. It's a unique and special setup, blessing and benefiting both the minister and his family and our mainly summertime community!

A couple of years ago, when one of the ministers was here, I felt "put off" by his demeanor and seeming disregard for some of the things I told him. Especially concerning how things needed to run during the week, as well as on Sunday during the service. We got through the week and weekend, and for the next couple of years, I stewed in my judgment of this minister, even talking to others on the mountain about my "concerns." Yes, gossip ensued because of me. Yet again, another reason for being ashamed of my behavior.

Then, another minister's name was submitted to me. He was a family member of the minister who had come two years before. The invitation for him to come for the week was made, but I was anticipating it not to go well, rerunning in my head the problems I'd dealt with before with his family member.

When Sunday came, I realized the first minister and his wife had traveled up also and were in attendance. I walked over, reintroducing myself, knowing it was the right thing to do. Almost immediately, the wife took me aside and confided in me with tears in her eyes that her husband had been diagnosed with Alzheimer's shortly after their visit two years prior. She told me she knew I had probably picked up some clues that something wasn't right back then. What wasn't right was that I made a judgment without ever thinking there could be a reason he didn't understand what I was asking of him. What wasn't right was me blabbing to others about this situation and putting doubt in others' minds about the character of this man.

Needless to say, I felt bad, and to be quite honest, as I write this, I still do. I've asked God for forgiveness and am trying to forgive myself too, vowing to use discernment, and ask God for wisdom before jumping to conclusions such as this ever again.

Time in the Truth

- **James 4:12**
- **Luke 6:31-37**
- **Matthew 7:1-5**
- **Matthew 6:9-15**
- **1 Samuel 16:7**
- **Romans 3:23-26**
- **John 8:1-11**
- **Mark 12:29-34**

Mirror Moment

Throwing a stone may be our worldly and human nature. However, it is NOT what God desires for us. How we so easily seem to slip into the habit of taking matters into our own hands, behaving poorly, and not consulting God is wrong. This causes conflict, division, heartache, and brokenness. The flip side is also true. If we choose instead to simply love and allow God to lead our steps, leaving judgment to Him, what freedom there is.

Ask yourself where you have placed yourself in the role of god. Surrender, ask forgiveness, and live in freedom! And be un-offendable!

Communion with my Creator

"Grant me, O Lord, to know what I ought to know, To love what I ought to love,

To praise what delights Thee most, to value what is precious in Thy sight, and to hate what is offensive to Thee. Do not suffer me to judge according to the hearing of the ears of ignorant men, but to discern with a true judgment between things visible and spiritual. And above all, always to inquire what is the good pleasure of Thy will. Amen"

—Thomas Kempis

Song Suggestions

Song Title	Artist
Jesus, Friend of Sinners	Casting Crowns
The Proof of Your Love	For King and Country

Theme

Assumptions, Judgmentalism

Discussion Questions following *Judgement Call Part 2: First Impressions*

1. Are you more apt to judge a book by its cover or read a bit of the story before making a judgment call?

2. Reflect on these questions before reading what God tells us about judging others.

   a. How does ignorance play into declaring judgment?

   b. How do assumptions add to the same?

   c. Why do we jump to conclusions quickly?

   d. What makes judging others a damaging practice?

   e. Are we supposed to judge at all? Is there ever a good time to judge?

3. Gossip was a result of my hasty judgment. How did that further ruin my witness as a believer? Where has gossip played a role in your own life? Has there been reconciliation?

4. Let's see directly what God says about judging:

   God is clear that judgment belongs to Him.

   Take a deep dive into the following verses, using the questions next to them for guidance: (You may want to pick and choose from these verses. Some may seem redundant.)

   James 4:12 How clear is it in this verse that we should not judge? What absolute word(s) are used to drive this point home even more?

   Luke 6:31-37 How do Jesus' own words bring even more conviction to the topic of us judging others? What are some practical ways we can apply this passage?

   Matthew 7:1-5 If we need any more clarification on how to treat those we would rather condemn with our judgments, these verses do just that. Using the idea of measurement from this passage, what are some ways we measure others that you may not have discussed yet?

   Define "hypocrisy." Looking closely at our lives, where has hypocrisy played a role in our behavior?

   Matthew 6:9-15 The Lord's Prayer + a lesson on forgiveness. How does embracing the words of the Lord's Prayer bring about humility and reason for us to take pause, reflecting on our sometimes high and mighty stature of judging? What does the lesson on forgiveness offer us if we have found ourselves caught in this snare?

   Galatians 1:10 How is "people pleasing" a part of our judgment of others?

   1 Samuel 16:7 Samuel was told by God that one of Jesse's sons would be the next king of Israel and to go anoint him. What did God tell Samuel he saw, versus what we see? Who was that king, and what number son was he? What more can we learn from this story?

Romans 3:23-26 Recognizing where we've acted as judge and jury should convict us and could also cause us to feel shame in how we've treated others. What do these verses provide in the way of hope? What qualities of God are discussed here that give us a second chance?

5. The event in **John 8:1-11** is powerful. How does Jesus respond to the judgment made by the hateful neighbors? What more can you learn from this story? And where in this story have you seen yourself?

6. As you close up this heavy discussion, what are we reminded of that is our main function as a follower of Christ in the greatest commandments ever given? Read **Mark 12:29-34**, then listen to the song suggestion as you meditate on the verses.

7. In closing today, you may choose to collectively read aloud the prayer from Thomas Kempis and add a sentence or two of your own.

    Details aren't necessary. "God knows them and the posture of your heart as you speak."

47. Hummingbirds

Hummingbirds are one of God's coolest creations, in my opinion. They are the smallest birds in the world, weigh less than a dime, can fly backwards, beat their wings 60–80 times per second, and have a heart that can exceed 1,200 beats per minute! Just stop and consider that for a second! What miracles in our own backyard!

Besides these amazing facts, hummingbirds are one of the earth's greatest pollinators! They are attracted to all vibrant colors, mainly bright reds and oranges. We have an abundance of hummingbirds that fly all around our area, even more if we put out feeders, have red geraniums, or simply wear red!

God created these birds to be attracted to the vivid colors so they would fulfill a much-needed part of the life cycle and spread of plants and flowers. We too, if we are attracted to the right things, fulfill a much needed purpose in this world. Spreading the love and good news of Jesus.

To unpack this, let's first look at how humans experience attractions. Some attractions can be good, some not so good, and others deadly. We must learn to be discerning in order to tell the difference. You see, if we aren't careful, our eyes can entice us, our ears desire to be tickled, our comfort can make us complacent, and our hunger can lead us astray.

There are so many voices, including our own, and many distractions that woo us and end up entangling us. Therefore, we must be vigilant and aware that many temptations exist all around us and know which voice or voices to listen to and which ones we should shut out!

If we were hummingbirds, how would we tell the difference between a red geranium and a brightly colored predator? The Wildlife Society tells us that hummingbirds have an outsized sense of smell that helps them make foraging decisions and stay out of danger, including dangerous insects and chemicals! Learning to "smell danger" in our lives is just as important.

← PHOTO I COULDN'T BELIEVE I WAS ABLE TO CAPTURE!
   IT HAPPENS OVER AND OVER ON OUR DECK!

This lesson reminds me of the very old Sunday School song called "Oh Be Careful Little Eyes What You See." It reminds us that God is Love and wants us to be careful about what we see, hear, say, and do, and where we go! It's very simplified, but a very real reminder that danger is present in our world, prowling around ready to devour us.

Don't let that happen!

Once we choose wisely which voices to listen to, just like humming-birds pollinate, (which means they transfer pollen grains from the male anther of a flower to the female stigma in order to create off-spring for the next generation), we too transfer and spread what is inside of us. This does and will affect the generations to come.

So, just as the hummingbirds discern where they should land in order to draw pollen and then disseminate it to other plants, we too should learn to be drawn to the Truth and then to spread that Truth and Love to others during this thing we call life on Earth.

Time in the Truth

- **Joshua 24:14-15; 23**
- **John 10:1-18**
- **1 Peter 5:6-8**
- **2 Corinthians 10:4, 5**
- ----------------------
- **Isaiah 61:1-2**
- **2 Corinthians 2:14-17**

- **Matthew 28:19, 20**
- **Mark 16:15**
- **Acts 1:7, 8; 4:19, 20**
- **Romans 1:16**
- **Isaiah 52:7**
- **Acts 28:30, 31**
- **Ephesians 4:11-16**

Mirror Moment

What vies for your attention? Where do you find yourself during your free time? Where do you spend your money? What apps and social media do you use most often, or what websites do you visit? The answers to these questions will reveal who and what receives your affections. How in line are they with what God wants for you, and where do adjustments need to be made?

How do the voices you listen to and the truth you choose for yourself bleed over into your sphere of influence? What should that look like today for you?

Communion with my Creator

Personalize this prayer by taking the time to consider what belongs in the blanks.

Dearest Attractor of My Soul,

Today I choose to place You on the throne of my Heart.

I admit I've been attracted to things that are dishonoring to You. I've spent way too much time _____. I have spent my resources on _____. I have watched and listened to _____, none of which are glorifying You.

Bring me back to my original desire to make You number One in my life, Father.

Give me discernment to know the difference between what is good and what is best for my life. Give me the boldness and the courage to fight the temptations in my life, which include _____.

And finally, as my ears become more attuned to You and I soak up the truth from the correct source, may my interactions, reactions, and responses spread to all those I have the privilege to reach. Passing along Jesus: an inheritance of love, compassion, goodness, and kindness.

In Jesus' name! Amen

Song Suggestions

Song Title	Artist
Speak	Bethany Music (Listening to God)
Guard Your Heart	Steve Green
Do Something	Matthew West (Legacy and Sharing Faith)

Theme

Our Attraction, Voices We Listen to AND

Sharing Faith, Evangelism

Side Note: This devotional actually has two parts. They can be done together or divided between two weeks of readings and questions.

Discussion Questions following *Hummingbirds*

1. Do you have a favorite bird? And if so, why?

2. Hummingbirds have a strong sense of smell that keeps them away from danger. What qualities should we all possess that "smell" danger and keep us safe?

3. We've talked in detail about discernment in a recent devo, so today in our group discussion we'll mainly be focusing on listening and "pollinating" our world with the Voice of God we've chosen to embrace.

    a. In **Joshua 24:14-15**, a question is posed. What is it, and what are the alternatives for us today? What does it mean to actually live out the phrase in the passage, "but as for me and my house, we will serve the Lord"? Verse 23 of the same chapter in Joshua will help in answering this question. Of course, use what we see as today's "foreign gods" in your discussion.

    b. Jesus, in **John 10:1-18**, paints a beautiful picture of listening for His voice. What are the metaphors used, and what do they mean for us today?

    c. The warning we are given in **1 Peter 5:6-8** is worthy of discussion. How do we recognize when the voices we hear are evil? Use **2 Corinthians 10:4, 5** to help you complete your answers.

4. Take five minutes and, using the prayer I wrote in the Communion With the Creator section, personally fill in the blanks.

    The next section of Discussion Questions refers to what we do with the Truth that has been entrusted to us! This can be done this week, or saved for another week.

5. Being a witness in our world by sharing the Good News of Jesus IS our key purpose in life. Can you recall a time when you had the opportunity to do this? Share boldly!

6. I may have gotten carried away with the next set of Scriptures, and honestly, I had to pare down from the enormity of verses on the topic of evangelism. Or as we'll call it from our hummingbird analogy, "pollinating our world"!!!

   Take time to read what you can, and discuss the importance of this role in our lives.

   Isaiah 61:1-2
   2 Corinthians 2:14-17
   Matthew 28:19, 20
   Mark 16:15
   Acts 1:7, 8; 4:19, 20
   Romans 1:16
   Isaiah 52:7
   Acts 28:30, 31
   Ephesians 4:11-16

7. Handing down our faith and love for Jesus in our world to our children, grandchildren, and friends couldn't be clearer to us throughout Scripture. Share some of the practical ways you have done this!

8. Finish up by thinking of those you should share God's message of hope and salvation with now. Pray for them by initials, by name, or silently as your leader guides the prayer! Then follow through. Their eternity might depend on it. You may be the only Jesus they ever see. Allow time to listen to a song suggestion!

48. Deep Wells

As we were in the process of purchasing our cabin, we discovered, through the necessary inspections, that the water well for the home was too close to our leach field. For those of you like me, prior to buying a cabin in the mountains, I had no idea what a bad situation that was. A leach field is where the black water from the bathroom goes to "live," causing some major contamination of our drinking water!! And **of course,** this was not ok!!!

The family who was selling the cabin chose to split the cost of the new well with us! We appreciated this gesture immensely!

What we **also** discovered, once the new well was complete was that the old well was much shallower AND barely put out enough water for cabin use. With the new well in great working order, these two revelations have now provided safe drinking water from a deep well AND a very good supply of water when we turn on the faucets!!

Let's stop for a moment and consider if we had remained oblivious to the way things were originally, how and what would have transpired. With no inspection, there would have been no new well to correct the issues. "Assuming" all was in good order, and being unaware of the issues, would have led to being satisfied with a trickle of water coming from our faucets, presuming that was "normal." **And** at the same time, being contaminated little by little from the leach field until we would have become sick. Too late to do anything. YIKES! Thank goodness for inspections and high standards in the USA!

Just like our water well, we too have "living wells" we draw from for wisdom, guidance, and knowledge to live our lives. Depending on how deep those wells are, what their origins are, and where they are placed will be evidenced in how we live. Regular inspections, evaluations, and adjustments to the well (translated as our hearts and minds) are a must if we are to continue to pursue the heart and mind of Christ in all our daily endeavors and relationships!

← WELLS MAY LOOK FAIRLY INSIGNIFICANT, YET THEIR PLACEMENT
  AND THEIR DEPTH ARE HIGHLY IMPORTANT!

If we don't stay vigilant, we can and probably will easily slip into believing half-truths, responding as we've always responded while using that as an excuse, and finding ourselves slipping backward little by little. Therefore, when it comes to what used to be an all-out passion for following our first love, Jesus, it ultimately becomes a complacent, stale faith, with little or no impact on our world or in our own lives!

Digging deep wells, with regular inspections, provides us with what we need to face all that is going on in our lives! If we rely on our status quo, we run the risk of becoming complacent (like just putting up with the old water well's output). We absolutely run the risk of our motives becoming impure (like the impure contaminated water), when what God wants for us is to push us to further depths in our relationship with Him and with others!

Time in the Truth

- **Psalm 1:1-3; 63:1-8**
- **Isaiah 41:17, 18; 55:1-6**
- **John 4:13-16; 14:6**

Mirror Moment

Consider the depth of your spiritual well. Are you drawing from old cisterns? OR are you creating space to dig deeper by reading, praying, listening, studying, being mentored, and memorizing? What can you and will you begin today, and stick with, that will renew your relationship with the perpetual Living Water as you pursue the Heart and Mind of Christ?

Communion with my Creator

Dear Living Water,

I must admit my well has somewhat run dry. I am not able to replenish for myself the depth I need to live even one day. Quench my thirst, my dry, parched spirit! Relieve, like only You can, the scorched places of my heart where I've relied on half-truths and old tapes in my head, becoming dull and even sick from the contamination of my flesh. Put me back on the track to draw deeply from Your truth and no one else's. I commit today to practice craving only Your goodness, Your Truth, Your guidance, and Your wisdom in ALL I say and do! Fill me abundantly and completely.

In Jesus' name! Amen

Song Suggestions

Song Title	Artist
Deep Cries Out	Bethel Music
River of Life	Mac Powell

Theme

Pursuing the Heart and Mind of Christ

Discussion Questions following *Deep Wells*

1. Have you ever been without water for any length of time? How does it feel? What is the importance of water for our physical bodies? The metaphor for spiritual dehydration is very similar in its effects! Read **Isaiah 41:17, 18**, which reminds us that God is always the answer to our spiritual thirst!

2. "Spiritual dryness happened when I was young, last year, last week, and even a few hours ago. It creeps in during seasons of suffering or celebration, seasons momentous or mundane, seasons of transition or waiting." –Maggie Combs

   What are your thoughts on this quote?

3. We all know the saying, "Doing the same thing and expecting different results is insanity." How does this phrase relate to our spiritual well-being as well? And what can we do if we want to guard against this? Read **Psalm 1:1-3** in order to gain wisdom in answering.

4. Read **Psalm 63:1-8**. What did David teach us when he was in a dry and desolate wilderness? What practices can we glean from David?

5. God's invitation to drink from His Living Water is for us all. Study the following verses in both the Old and New Testaments, finding the common threads. **Isaiah 55:1-6** and **John 4:13-16**.

6. Where do you feel there is only a trickle of water to quench your spiritual thirst today? And where are you being convicted of being contaminated by the world? Be specific, such as "I lack patience with...", or "I feel anger toward...", or "My relationship with _____ isn't what it needs to be," or "I don't feel God's presence like I used to..." Either share out loud OR write it down for further examination.

7. The soil of our lives can and does crack from spiritual malnutrition. To paraphrase a devotional I read recently, which convicted me: "Reading God's word isn't drinking it," and "Skimming God's Word doesn't quench our thirst." I could also add that going to church doesn't make us holy, reciting obligatory prayers doesn't transform or prepare us, and going through any Christian rituals won't equip us for the battle of life! If so, what will? Which one of these sentences speaks to you?

   The simplest answer is sometimes the best... "Return to Your First Love" - Pursuing the Heart and Mind of Christ!

8. Along with the true confessions from question six and the "simple answer" above, come up with specifics. How do you personally plan to dig deeper wells in order to pursue the Heart and Mind of Christ?!

9. Listen to one of the song suggestions and pray to close out your group session!!

49. Wind*

One of my favorite sounds from the mountain is the wind blowing through the trees. You can hear the rustling of the leaves, the rumble of the branches, and occasionally, the thunder before the storm peeks over the mountaintop. Wind can be a very scary thing, or it can be a very peaceful thing... To me, it's all about perspective.

Wind, tornadoes, and hurricanes—those can be destructive and damaging. To be quite honest, my life, prior to a few short years ago, was consumed with damaging wind. The wind of chaos, abuse, and horror. The wind of my world was all-consuming, dark, and full of terror.

But God.

I will never forget my first trip to the cabin. I found myself in this beautiful place, surrounded by the incredible scenery, and I began to feel peace. I didn't know at the time what it was, but I do now. It was the peace of the Holy Spirit. The peace of the fresh wind that only He can bring. That week was in March 2020, just as the world began to shut down due to COVID-19. My sweet Mama and I spent ten or so days tucked away in the little cabin in the mountain, and I began to learn how to breathe, how to relax. I remember telling her that I'd never known how to relax before. My entire nervous system, due to years of abuse and torture prior to being adopted at the age of 30, was constantly on high alert. We sat on the deck, took hikes, read, sang, danced, laughed, cried, yelled (not at each other, but at the enemy), painted nails, stargazed, and breathed. She taught me how to breathe. 1...2...3. Take in a deep breath as you count to three and let it out. We still use "123" to this day, when needed.

Wind—the wind of God—the breath of God... YHWH. Yahweh. When Moses asked God what His name was, God responded (in Hebrew), "Yhwh." Scholars report that these two consonants represent the sounds we make when we breathe. Inhaling: yh; exhaling: wh. This means that every human being, whether they choose to believe in Him or not, speaks His name with every breath they take.

His breath is what fills our lungs. His breath is what gives us our very existence and our very being.

Let's do it together now, ready?

Breathe in and count...

1.....

2.....

3.....

Exhale...

Biblically, "fresh wind" represents the Holy Spirit. One of the things the Holy Spirit does in our lives is to help bring about change, transformation, and newness. He can breathe fresh life and fresh breath upon the dry, cracked, broken, and hurting places in our lives and bring us to a place of healing, freedom, redemption, and transformation.

What do you need in your life? Where do you need fresh wind? Maybe it's as simple as taking a deep breath. Maybe it's a career change. Maybe it's seeking out counseling to begin to heal from past traumas. Ask Him. Let Him breathe a fresh wind upon your life.

Wind doesn't have to be scary—it can be healing and life-giving.

One more time, all together.

Breathe in...

1...

2...

3...

Exhale...

You are loved. Wholly and fully loved.

---

*This devotional was written and shared by one of my daughters, Audrey. Thank you dear, for your beautiful words.

Time in the Truth

- **Genesis 2:7**
- **John 20:22**
- **Isaiah 40:31**
- **Psalm 150:6**

Mirror Moment

When you think about the "wind" in your life right now, does it feel chaotic and destructive, or peaceful and life-giving? Why?

Where do you most need the "fresh wind" of the Holy Spirit to bring renewal or healing?

What is one area of your life where you've been holding your breath—spiritually, emotionally, or physically—and need to exhale in trust?

How can you create moments this week to intentionally pause, breathe, and invite God's presence into your day?

When you breathe in and out, how does it change your perspective to remember that you are speaking God's name with every breath?

Communion with my Creator

Lord Yahweh,

With every breath I take, I speak Your holy name.
You are the One who formed me from the dust, breathed life into my lungs, and gave me my being.
You are the wind in the trees, the whisper in the stillness, and the mighty rushing wind that brings power and transformation.

I confess that in the past, the winds in my life have felt chaotic and destructive: storms of pain, fear, and brokenness.
But You, Lord, have shown me another wind:
Your wind of peace.
Your breath of healing.
Your Spirit brings newness and hope.

Holy Spirit, I invite You now; blow over the dry, weary places in my soul.
Breathe life into the parts of me I thought were beyond repair.
Quiet the inner storms and replace them with the peace that surpasses understanding.
Teach me to inhale Your presence and exhale fear, anxiety, and lies.

Lord, let Your fresh wind move me into healing, into freedom, into the wholeness You desire for me.
Shift my perspective so I see that wind does not have to destroy...
It can carry me, lift me, and remind me of Your constant presence.

Even in the stillness of the mountain or the chaos of the valley, help me remember:
I am loved.
Wholly.
Completely.
Forever.

In the name of Yahweh, Amen

Song Suggestions

Song Title	Artist
Great Are You Lord	All Sons & Daughters
Rest on Us	Maverick City Music & Upper Room

Theme

Holy Spirit, Fresh Wind, Fresh Life

Discussion Questions following *Wind**

1. Where is the windiest place you've ever been? Describe the feeling. Was there exhilaration or fear?

2. When you think of "wind" in your life now, does it feel chaotic and destructive, or peaceful and life-giving? Why? Consider the driving power from the "wind" of both scenarios in your life.

3. After carefully reading **Genesis 2:7**, discuss the significance of God breathing life into Adam and into us. How should understanding "becoming a living person" impact our lives?

4. With the idea of powerful wind in mind, read **Isaiah 40:28-31**. Unpack the possibilities described within these verses: from going it alone to mounting up with wings like Eagles. What adjectives are used to describe the youths and the vigorous young men? What transformation occurs when God is added to the equation?

5. From the passage in Genesis that we read in question #3, fast-forward to **John 20:22** where Jesus breathes a new reality onto His apostles. What does His breath bring them now? What force is now available to them and to us when we surrender and exchange our strength for His?

6. Where do you most need the "fresh wind" of the Holy Spirit to bring renewal or healing? Is there an area of your life where you've been holding your breath and need to exhale? This could be spiritual, emotional, or physical.

7. Put your heads together as a group to come up with some practical ways to create moments this week to intentionally invite the Holy Spirit's presence into your day. Ideas can include pausing and breathing, but please add more.

8. Re-read the paragraph that explains "Yhwh" as signifying breath. When you breathe in and out, how does it change your perspective to remember that you are speaking God's name with every breath? Then take a few breaths together with this thought in mind.

9. If discussing the Holy Spirit is fairly new to you, and you don't understand how He works in our lives, read **John 3:1-21**. This is an encounter between Nicodemus, a leader in the Jewish faith, and Jesus. Jesus helps him better understand the mystery of how God is moving. Draw links between wind and breath and the Holy Spirit, especially in **verse 8**. I believe there will always be an element of mystery until we get to Heaven. Hoping and trusting in the power of the Holy Spirit is part of our faith.

10. End with prayer, **Psalm 150:6**, and one of the suggested songs.

50. Road 9

Our little community was first settled in the 1930s. The land was plotted out, and people began purchasing the lots and building their cabins over the next several decades. The roads were planned out several years after the land was plotted, which means that all the roads on the mountain cross over people's property, and are therefore owned by the land/cabin owners. It is imperative that everyone is cooperate and allow easement across their property for others to get to their land and cabins. However, there are those owners who are less than happy when others cross their stretch of land to get to their own property, and this has caused "human friction," as you can imagine. It's called life.

Road 9, a "major" thoroughfare and the only connection from one side of the mountain to the other, goes *directly* over *our* property. We actually own that portion of the road! We've often joked about how we could erect a toll booth during the busier summer months and make a pretty good profit. Hehe... JK! Everyone is welcome to cross. But only some are invited to sit and stay for a while. More on that in a few.

There is a person who also owns a portion of 9 (less traveled than ours on the backside of the mountain) who has actually erected signs "prohibiting anyone to cross" over his portion of the road, and thus causing the landowners on the other side of him to take an alternate and longer route.

Both of these situations bring to mind a couple words of importance in our lives... "access" and "trespass." If we treated the road in front of our cabin as a trespass and didn't allow access across our property, those with cabins on the backside of the mountain would be inhibited from reaching home. And with the signs on the other man's property (however illegal that is) scaring anyone from passing, it does just that... frightens anyone who dares pass by, and I assume, causes some strife in relationships with his neighbors.

← YOU'LL FIND OUR CABIN RIGHT AROUND THE NEXT BEND IN THE ROAD!

How we learn to trust others and give access, or not, in our relationships is a bit more complex than a road laid out in front of us, but it can give us a good place to begin this discussion! Allowing connection to a portion of ourselves doesn't mean we must allow complete access to ALL of us. Allowing cars to drive over our land doesn't mean we provide access to our deck, our kitchen, or our closets. It simply allows access to a portion of what we own. On the flip side, never allowing any access because we struggle with trusting others, likely due in part to hurts from the past, isn't healthy either. This kind of living is similar to not allowing cars to drive by, or by placing signs that scare even the neighbors from attempting to get to the land they own.

This is where healthy balance and healthy boundaries are crucial and should be well thought through. If someone isn't healthy enough to have full access to our hearts or has trespassed on us in the past, then we should, by all means, be cautious about protecting ourselves. Some of us easily give trust, whereas others of us are wary and only give trust if it's well earned. I'm not saying either is bad or good; it depends on our nature, as well as our experiences.

Experience, as helpful as it can be in this area, can also color, or taint, the value of trust. Guarding our hearts from those who are trustworthy can and usually does end up affecting our close relationships. What I believe we should add to experience is wisdom. Wisdom can bring us much clarity on this subject. With wisdom comes understanding of why we easily distrust, and it potentially can help us find the root cause. Once we do that, healing has a chance to bring us to a more informed view of trusting others. This restoration, in turn, can bring us hope and take us to a place where we are not so walled in or guarded. With wisdom comes discernment, which helps us to decipher whether or not access should be given at all or completely denied. There are situations and trespasses that have occurred where denied access is the correct response, because mending a relationship is beyond repair or because there was abuse involved.

It is complicated. And I don't want to assume a short devotional can do much to solve all the complex scenarios. Let this be the beginning of your journey to understanding. For further investigation, PLEASE check out *Boundaries*, by Henry Cloud (recommended in an earlier devo), AND Lysa Terkheurst's *Good Boundaries and Goodbyes*. They have been incredible resources for me and others I love.

Our small patch of road is open to all who drive past. And more often than not, when we are there, we stop and talk, or at least wave, to those passing by, sometimes even inviting them up to our deck for a glass of tea and to sit a spell. This gesture has the potential to deepen relationships and trust. Sadly, the other gentleman's signs are a roadblock, allowing only for fear and potential anger.

Time in the Truth

- **Proverbs 25:28**
- **Proverbs 4:20–23**
- **John 15:12-17**
- **Romans 12:9-21**

- **Acts 15:36-41**
- **2 Timothy 4:11**
- **Colossians 3:15**
- **Philippians 4:7**

Mirror Moment

Which "portion of the road" do you own? The one that allows passersbys, or the one with the "No Access" sign.

I highly recommend reading the books I mentioned in the devotional for much deeper study on healthy boundaries and the need for them!

Communion with my Creator

Dear Architect of Boundaries,

Oh Lord, I want to trust You completely! I desire openness and transparency with You Father. And because You are trustworthy, I also want to learn from You how to be open to others with clarity. Wisdom and discernment come from You. Give me discernment to assess my relationships and the access I allow them into my life. Teach me wisdom to construct healthy boundaries so as to protect my heart, as well as others! And above all teach me to love like You do!

In Jesus' name! Amen

Song Suggestions

Song Title	Artist
No Longer Slaves	Bethel Music
Fear Is a Liar	Zach Williams

Theme

Access to Our Hearts, Boundaries

Side note: Cattle Guards, an earlier devotional, covered the importance of healthy boundaries. As I've stated before, repetition over some topics can be helpful. I hope you will learn something new from this one.

Discussion Questions following *Road 9*

1. Do you like to travel? If so, what is your favorite way to travel? Why? Tell about a road trip you took and what it was like traveling that way. What have you learned about yourself when traveling?

2. Define the words "trespass" and "access" in the context of roads. Which one of these words comes to mind more easily when you think of your life?

3. **Proverbs 25:28** gives us a good picture of what our lives resemble when we have no boundaries. Discuss a city without walls, especially in Old Testament times, and how this relates to living... Focus on the second half of this verse. How important is self-control to forming boundaries? How can **Proverbs 4:20-23** deepen your discussion about the need for protecting your heart?

4. After reading **John 15:12-17**, discuss how loving others could appear to be in opposition to setting boundaries. What, if any, is the struggle here between the two? Why does it sometimes seem antithetical to love and place boundaries?

5. Continuing with this line of questioning, of placing boundaries and being loving, read Romans **12:9-21**. What words or phrases in this passage complement the idea of having borders? Think on the phrase in **verse 18**, "as far as it depends on you." How could the following commentary on this set of verses help? "Believers do good even to people who cause harm. Believers trust God to bring judgment against people who are doing evil. This is because only God's love is strong enough to stop the power of evil." –Biblica Study Bible.

6. If time allows, do a character study of the players in **Acts 15:36-41**. What did you learn? The disagreement here was between Paul and Barnabas. They argued and then separated. Then the Holy Spirit continued working through both men to spread the message about Jesus. Later, one of Paul's letters shows that Paul, Mark, and Barnabas became friends once again, working together to strengthen God's church. Read **2 Timothy 4:11**. Is there a time when this type of relationship has played out in your life?

7. One of the positive results of healthy boundaries, whether it means some access to your heart or hard stops of no trespassing, is the peace that comes from them. What are your thoughts on this idea?

   Read and place your own name in **Colossians 3:15** and **Philippians 4:7**.

8. Enjoy one of the song suggestions and pray as you finish your time together.

51. Virgin Snow: Sacred Moments in Life

Winter in the mountains has an entirely different feel from the summertime. I receive different types of "nourishment" from each season. What the winter has provided when I've bundled up to walk or snowshoe through the deep snow is an incredible sense of the depth, wonder, and presence of God. From the snow glistening, resembling thousands of priceless diamonds, like a snow blanket undisturbed before my eyes, to the silence of the falling snow... I'm not only reminded of the profound richness of this sight but also of actually experiencing Holy Ground. I'm awestruck by God's Holiness and His purity. This scene causes me to stop dead in my tracks. These encounters often catch me off guard. They are sacred moments in my life. Sacred, a hallowed presence connecting me to Almighty God. Those moments when you know God has gone before to prepare this space and place for you to experience. I don't take these brushes with The Almighty lightly. I feel I've been invited into an extraordinary glimpse of His Majesty. Its impact on my life was powerful and life-changing, beyond anything words can easily or ever describe.

My portion of today's devotional ends here. And it's where yours begins. Check out the Mirror Moments and go from there!

Time in the Truth

- Exodus 3:14
- Deuteronomy 4:7-9
- Isaiah 43:10-13; 44:6-8; 45:21; 66:1, 2
- Psalm 139:7-12
- 2 Peter 3:8, 9
- Ephesians 4:1-7

← NOTHING QUITE LIKE A MORNING SNOW COVERING THE TREES AND MOUNTAINS.

Mirror Moment

When have you experienced a life-altering sacred moment? Write about it now, describing not only the "feels" BUT even more importantly, the awe-struck wonder and attributes of God you've recognized from those moments. Use the Scriptures provided to identify those attributes if you need, and look up more! Just Google "the attributes of God" and be astounded. And don't shy away from pouring out your praise, your awe, and your tears to Him.

The song suggestions for this devotional are endless. I apologize if I may have gotten too carried away. Use some of them to enhance your time today and later this week as you stay focused on God.

Communion with my Creator

Dear Hallowed One,

The purpose of my prayer today is to bring You worship. Opening my heart and life to recognize Your Worth and Your Glory! Adoring You, revering You, the Almighty Sovereign, the I AM. Giving You all my devotion and respect. As I read Your Word and discover more of Your Greatness, I make them my prayer of adoration. Thank You for the sacred moments You've allowed me to experience.

In Jesus' name! Amen

Song Suggestions

Song Title	Artist
Holy Ground	Charity Gayle
Agnus Dei	Mathew W. Smith
How Great is Our God	CeCe Winans
Be Still	Kari Jobe
Revelation	Kari Jobe
Is He Worthy?	Andrew Peterson/Chris Tomlin
God of Wonders	Third Day
Oceans	Hillsong United
Blessings	Laura Story
Come to the Table	Sidewalk Prophets
Indescribable	Chris Tomlin
I Need Thee Every Hour	Hymns of Grace
Holy, Holy, Holy	Audrey Assad

Theme
Sacred Moments, The Awe of God

Discussion Questions following *Virgin Snow: Sacred Moments in Live*

1. Define the word "sacred," paying close attention to the synonyms of the word. Discuss these words and personalize their meaning.

2. Can you think of a time in your life when a holy moment happened to you? What were the circumstances, and how did it impact your life?

3. Putting God on the throne of our lives and keeping Him there forever is not an easy task. The world, its distractions, and its enticements often prey on our attention, as we've talked about before. When you read today's

passages, prepare yourself to soak in the enormity of God, declaring He is the One and Only. Open with a prayer for understanding. As you dig into the Scriptures for today, consider what they say about the Sovereignty of God and the awe that we should have for Him daily.

Choose individual words or phrases to contemplate and meditate on from the following verses. When it comes to how you view God in your daily life, how does He want to shift your ordinary to become extraordinary today and every day?

Exodus 3:14: What did God call Himself? What power is behind those words? Who was He speaking to, and what were the circumstances surrounding this encounter? Have you had a burning bush experience?

Deuteronomy 4:7-9: When have you experienced the nearness of God? What is the warning given in verse 9, and how does this apply today?

Isaiah 43:10-13; 44:6, 8; 45:21: What does God declare about Himself in these passages? And when you perceive the word "eternity," how does it put present things into perspective? How does your life have an eternal perspective, or does it?

Isaiah 66:1, 2: As you stop to consider God's description of Himself here, we may think, *How do we possibly matter to Him?* However, how does He conclude verse 2; what does He want from us?

Psalm 139:7-12: How does reading this passage bring hope to believers and provoke fear in those who don't?

Ephesians 4:1-7: How do these words in the New Testament make the Oneness of God even more personal to those of us who live as Jesus followers?

4. Being attuned to the Spirit and expectant of Him in your life often ignites sacred moments. Spend some time talking about being attuned to the Spirit and what that looks like.

5. Prayer suggestion: Close out by praying this short-phrase prayer: Have one person start and another designated to close. Everyone simply says and finishes the sentence: "God, You are ____, and in my life You are _____."

6. As time permits, choose some of the song suggestions to enrich your study together. You could also listen to a different song after each discussion question.

52. More Bears in our Neighborhood

Some at 64 years old would consider winding down to sit in the rocker on the front porch, sipping tea, and reminiscing. Don't get me wrong, I love my glider and drinking my morning tea, overlooking the mountains and trees, remembering the past, and resting. But at the same time, I wonder, *Is God truly done with me OR YOU until this heart stops beating, and we have the awesome privilege to sit face to face with the Savior, sipping whatever amazing drink Heaven has to offer?* I think not. But either fear or complacency, or perhaps burnout and lack of motivation, would like us to remain seated.

The bears around our area have made for a pretty big presence in the summertime over the last few years. They seem less bothered by people and have frightened cabin owners into staying inside the safety of their four walls, only venturing out to their front yards. Living in fear of what MIGHT happen, or even the likelihood of encountering a bear, would keep us from experiencing this mountain and all it has to offer. Now, going out unprepared isn't wise either. I've addressed the need for preparation in an earlier devotional, "Be Prepared." So, I prepare, and then I choose not to sit around waiting until the potential danger passes. Isn't that exactly what we'd be doing if we didn't find a passion in life or refuel to keep moving forward, propelling us to be purposeful and productive even though it may look different than in our younger years?

Scripture tells us that the opposite of fear is love. Where fear paralyzes and keeps us stuck, love propels us to act, responding to the life flow inside of us. *Love needs to overcome our fears. Unfortunately, it's often the other way around. Love gets lost because of our fears.*

God wants us to remain fruitful, period. And with added wisdom, because of experiences and lessons we've learned, we can use gifts that have been sharpened over the years to pursue, and better, the little corner of our world. Or maybe even choose to learn new and exciting things we never dared dream of when we were raising

← PHOTO TAKEN BY A FRIEND, BRENDA TRAFTON, NEAR HER CABIN
IN A NEIGHBORING MOUNTAIN COMMUNITY.

237

a family and just making ends meet. Mine certainly has looked different from what I did earlier on in my life as a teacher, but certainly still remains true to my calling and passion. That of loving, caring, and walking with people God has placed in my life to places of healing, peace, and freedom, **all with His help, of course, and pointing to Him!**

One of the purposes of writing my thoughts in a book was to share my experiences so you could relate and find more joy, peace, and purpose in your journey of life. Like I mentioned way back in my opening, I had this dream since I was about 12. That was over 50 years ago! This journey has taken quite a long time. A friend once gave me a small plaque that read, "The Joy is in the Journey." Is that the case with you?

Another purpose of writing this book became clear while writing. Fighting the horrors of human trafficking has been something I have had a passion for ever since I heard about it, but I didn't know how. After watching the amazing movie on the subject, *Sound of Freedom*, I was moved to find a way to actually help. This movie, along with the book *The Well-Lived Life* written by 102-year-old Gladys McGrary, MD, emphasizes how we can't stop living just because we aren't as young as we used to be; both helped me realize that no "bear"—big, small, imagined, or otherwise—could take away my desire to help in this fight. A portion of the sales, or donations, from *Lessons From the Mountain* will go toward the fight for the freedom of anyone enslaved in these horrors.

If you feel you've stopped making a difference, don't remain seated. Get up and start moving and doing life again! Find your passion and continue to use your God-given gifts and talents to make a difference!

Time in the Truth

- **Ephesians 6:18-20**
- **Matthew 28:18-20**
- **Romans 12:2-8**
- **Ephesians 2:10**
- **John 15:8**
- **1 Corinthians 3:16**
- **Hebrews 10:24, 25**
- **Psalm 90:12**

Mirror Moment

What bear are you staring down?

What makes you so righteously angry that you have to act?

Don't rock in your rocker any longer, or live on just the memories of past glory moments. Take a stand, and find a way to make a difference. You get to decide today!

I have no idea what difference I'll make with this book, but it won't keep me from trying.

Thank you for taking your precious time to read these learned lessons. I hope and pray they will or have inspired you, invigorated you, and catapulted you to do greater things to change your world and glorify God in the doing of it.

Communion with my Creator

Dear Passion Giver,

Continue to guide my steps here on Earth. Take away any worry that makes me want to flee. Any anxiety that makes me want to freeze. And any fear that makes me want to fight. Instead, fill me with the courage to live boldly for You. Continue to show me the way You want me to go. Give me a passion to reach the potential You originally created for me to live out. I may only be one, but with Your Presence living within me, anything is possible. I want to live fully abandoned for YOU ALONE!

In Jesus' name! Amen

Song Suggestions

Song Title	Artist
More to this Life	Steven Curtis Chapman
Finish Well	Karen Peck & New River

Theme

Facing Our Fears, Living Boldly for the Kingdom,
Stepping Out of Our Comfort Zone

Side Note: A book I read when I was about 13 solidified my faith, particularly one chapter. The book is entitled More Than a Carpenter. It is still in print, and I highly recommend it! Chapter 7 is entitled "Who Would Die for a Lie?" After reading that chapter, I was convinced Jesus was real, and everything in Scripture was true!

The apostles never stopped serving their Lord until they (all but John) were martyred.

Discussion Questions following *More Bears in our Neighborhood*

1. What do the "bears" in your life look like? What has kept you "seated"?

2. Do you feel like you are aimless or adrift? If you've felt this way in the past, what helped you become motivated again?

3. If you're in your older years reading this book, how have your passions and giftedness changed over the years? What role does age play in the way we live our lives?

4. A great example of someone who didn't stop ministering and writing is the Apostle Paul. He wrote at least four of his epistles while he was under house arrest, before he was murdered for his love and devotion to Jesus. Read **Ephesians 6:18-20**. Is there an example of a person you know who, even when they were elderly, never stopped using their gifts and ministering?

5. **Matthew 28:18-20** is often referred to as the Great Commission. These are some of the final words recorded that Jesus spoke to his apostles. How powerful have they been in your life so far, and what can they mean for your life starting today?

6. After Jesus' ascension, how seriously did His apostles follow the Great Commission? With their leader no longer with them, they could have all gone back to the way their lives were before they knew Jesus. *But none of them did.* Why do you think that was?

   Do a quick ChatGPT or some other search service on how the apostles died. Take a few minutes to discuss what you find. (See my note at the end of this devo that was a turning point in my life.) At any time in their lives, they could have probably saved their own by denouncing Jesus. But they didn't. The tough question for us might be, how have we denounced Him by not continuing to serve and minister while we are able?

7. **Romans 12:2-8**. How does your life reflect using your gifts?

8. After reading **Ephesians 2:10** and **John 15:8**, take a minute to share how His workmanship—YOU—is created to do more for Him. And what that might look like.

9. If you come to the place of "I can't anymore" or "I don't know what to do," how does **1 Corinthians 3:16** change the equation?

10. If you feel "your day drawing nearer," how does the truth stated in **Hebrews 10:24, 25** pour courage into you?

11. Being mindful of how our days on this planet are limited, what can we glean from **Psalm 90:12**? Pray, and listen to one of the songs as you close.

53. Dead Ends

A very dear friend who visited our cabin was determined to find Barbara's Bench. She had read about it in my very first devotional and wanted to find it for herself. She had been there with me in the past, guiding us to it, but this was the first time she was "on her own," seeking for herself the comfort of the bench and the beauty seen from it. On her way, she encountered a handmade sign that read, "Dead End." She was certain the bench was on that road, so she proceeded cautiously, optimistic about reaching her destination. Not knowing where she would end up, she had doubts, peppered with fear of getting lost. She had also forgotten to take her water and therefore, was parched and very hot. However, she was determined, and at every bend in the road, she had high hopes that soon she would discover "my" sacred spot that inspired me to write *Lessons From the Mountain*. She eventually DID find the bench and proudly sent me a selfie with the sign that reads, "Barbara's Bench"!

Haven't we all seen those "Dead End" signs in our lives? Stop to consider where they originated? I believe some come from noises and voices that keep us from experiencing the life God planned for us. Some may be well-intentioned, but not at all God's divine plan. Are those handmade signs made by those who want to disillusion us or distract us from what God has intended? Or are those truly coming from godly advisors and Scripture? How we respond to those signs will ultimately result in where we end up! Finding our Barbara's Bench, or somewhere lost.

That handmade sign was a distraction to my friend, a way of trying to keep her from reaching her destination. However, she was unwavering in her pursuit, resolute until she found what she was looking for! This, too, my friends, is what happens when we don't listen to the sound of the noisy gong and clanging cymbal that would deter us. We must choose instead to recognize and listen to the voice of the One who first formed us, then paved out the perfect plan for who we were supposed to become and what He had for us to accomplish here on Earth. He has a plan to walk with us to push through that darkness, root out all lies ever spoken to

← SHOULD WE ALWAYS BELIEVE A SIGN—ESPECIALLY A HANDMADE
   DEAD END SIGN, IF GOD HAS MORE FOR US?

us, bring to our attention our own blind spots, support us on the journey of healing, and then, with His power and guidance, bring us to the place where we belong! The journey isn't always easy. It can be exhausting, and the signs are not always clear. But, if we know Him and His Word, and we trust His voice, we will be on the road to where we belong, and we will be reminded that the journey in finding that destination is as important as the final destination itself.

The friend who encouraged me to write this particular devotional helped me push through a period of darkness, a dead end of sorts, in my own life, and helped me reach the other side. The Barbara Bench side! Her consistent prayers, her patient and understanding manner, and her godly wisdom from facing a similar situation, provided me clarity to recognize that the handmade sign reading "Dead End" was a lie. She also held me accountable, helping me to see where I had blind spots regarding the situation. Whatever challenges you face, whatever lies you may have believed OR even spoken over yourself, are NOT God's truth.

As I prepare to close this set of simply shared *Lessons from the Mountain*, I pray for all who choose to read, that in your reading, you have found a deeper walk with Jesus and continue on the path that leads to Barbara's Bench.

*Side Note: Bonus read! As you read this devotional, you likely recognized elements of several previous ones. The message of this devo echoes and summarizes the purpose of the entire project. I hope you will agree. Thank you, Lisa Blake, for suggesting I write one last devotional on the lie of Dead Ends.

Time in the Truth

- **Psalm 32:8, 9**
- **Psalm 119:17-40**
- **Romans 12:1, 2**
- **Philippians 3:8-21**

- **Ephesians 1:7-12**
- **Psalms 25:4, 5**
- **Proverbs 3:5-13**

Mirror Moment

Consider what you may be facing that leads to a dead-end sign. Is that dead-end thinking of your own making, prompted by fears, uncertainty, and doubt? What brought you to that place? What choices do you find yourself making that lead you to that sort of thinking instead of relying on God to show you the best pathway ahead? How might your blind spots play a role in moving forward? Be honest with yourself, and then allow God to walk alongside you to transform you into the best possible version of you!

Communion with my Creator

Dear Dead-End Breaker, Blind-Spot Revealer, Path Finder, and Way Maker,

"I've been told that there is nothing that can be done, that I've run out of options, that I've hit a dead end. But I know that You, Lord, are endless, timeless, all-knowing, and all-loving. I know too that in every moment of life there is grace and light. Please, Lord, bring me Your wisdom and patience. Fill my heart with hope that rests in You and Your Salvation. Make Your way, which has no end, clear to me and all those upon whom I rely. And help me to rest in the truth, 'With God, all things are possible.'"

In Jesus' name! Amen

Prayer borrowed from Maureen Pratt

Song Suggestions

Song Title	Artist
Way Maker	Michael W. Smith
Red Sea Road	Ellie Holcomb

Theme

Determination, Recognizing Blind Spots,
Fighting Through the Darkness

Discussion Questions following *Dead Ends*

1. What is the first thing that pops into your head when you think of the words "dead end"?

2. Open today's discussion by reading and answering the questions posed in the Mirror Moment. Stop and listen to "Red Sea Road", by Ellie Holcomb.

3. After reading **Psalm 32:8, 9**, consider how ego, pride, and doing things the same way we always have led to dead-end thinking in **verse 9**, and how learning what **verse 8** provides counteracts those negative paths. Especially focus on the verbs in **verse 8**.

4. No one I know likes to talk about blind spots, except maybe when they refer to someone else. But with your own blind spots in mind, how does the passage in **Psalm 119:17-40** benefit us in addressing our own blind spots? Find the phrases the psalmist uses where we may not see clearly. Follow your discussion of this passage by reading **Romans 12:1, 2**. In these verses, how does the transformative power of God break through our now-recognized blind spots and keep us from staying stuck on our dead-end path?

5. Read **Philippians 3:8-21** and **Ephesians 1:1-12**. With your blind spots no longer blinding you and your determination to live a life worthy of God's calling for you, how can these words from Paul encourage your faith and make obedience a joy from this day forward as we "eagerly wait for a Savior, the Lord Jesus Christ, who will transform the body of our lowly condition into conformity with His glorious body..."?

6. Use the following verses as your prayer, personalizing them with your name. **Psalm 25:4, 5**, and **Proverbs 3:5-13**. Close by listening to Way Maker.

The Climb Home

Our cabin sits at 8,792 feet. Eagle Nest, just three miles down the mountain, rests at 8,241 feet.

That's a 551-foot difference. Not the steepest incline, but for this flatland girl, hiking it on foot is no small task—especially when the air starts thinning and each breath takes a little more effort.

In a car, you hardly notice the climb. But on foot—well, that's another story. Each step reminds you that progress costs something. The higher you go, the more it requires.

I've often thought about how that little stretch of mountain is a picture of life. It takes effort to make a marriage last. Effort to raise kids with character. Effort to walk in truth, to forgive, to stay kind, to keep showing up when you're tired. These things don't happen by accident—they take intention, endurance, and heart.

We don't talk about "effort" much anymore. It's not a popular word in a world that looks for shortcuts. But real growth—the kind that changes us—takes work. It takes digging in, pushing through, and leaning hard on the One who gives us strength.

I decided one day to actually count the steps from Eagle Nest up to our cabin. There were 7,623 of them. I can't tell you how many times I had to stop, catch my breath, and convince myself to keep going. Some stretches were easy; others felt endless. But step by step, I made it. And every few hundred steps, the view changed—just a little at first, then dramatically as I got closer to the top.

Isn't that how our walk with God works? Some days we move forward with energy and confidence. Other days it's slow going—one small act of faith at a time. But even then, He's right there beside us, steadying our steps and reminding us that the climb is worth it.

Each of those 7,623 steps reminds me of the lessons in these pages—lessons from creation, from stillness and storms, from laughter and lament. Every devotional has been like one step upward—each with its own view, its own challenge, its own glimpse of God's handiwork.

And just like the climb, none of it is wasted.

When I finally reach the cabin, lungs burning and legs trembling, I always turn to look back. The road below doesn't seem quite as daunting anymore. What once felt impossible now feels sacred. Every pause, every prayer, every moment of effort brought me higher—closer not only to the cabin, but closer to the Lord who met me along the way.

So, as you close this book, my prayer is simple: keep climbing. Keep trusting. Keep taking the next faithful step. The path may be steep, and the air may thin at times, but the view—the view from the top—is worth every bit of the effort.

Because in the end, it's not just about reaching the cabin. It's about who we become, and Who we've walked with, on the way there.

Thank you for the opportunity you've allowed me to share with you the lessons I have learned from my little piece of paradise. I pray each and every one of you finds the Only Source of truth, peace, and joy, and most of all, the Love of Jesus! He is worth it, and so are you!

A Blessing for the Journey

May your own climb be filled with wonder, courage, and grace.
May you pause often to catch your breath, to notice beauty, and to thank the One who walks beside you.
And when you reach your own "cabin" moments—the quiet places where you finally rest—may you look back with gratitude for every step that brought you there.

Keep your eyes lifted, your heart steady, and your faith alive.
"I lift up my eyes to the hills—where does my help come from?
My help comes from the Lord, the Maker of heaven and earth."
— **Psalm 121:1–2**

The journey is uphill... But oh, the view is glorious.

Step Deeper Into the Lessons!

Scan the QR code to explore a gallery of photos that bring each lesson to life! Access heartfelt testimonials and fresh insights I'll be sharing in the weeks and months ahead. Keep checking back—there's always more to learn from the mountain!

LessonsFromTheMountain.com

← PHOTO TAKEN RIGHT AFTER WE PURCHASED THE CABIN
  DREAMING OF ALL THE ADVENTURES WE WOULD HAVE TOGETHER.

Letter to my Readers and a Personal Thanks

God nudged me to write this book for as long as I can remember. But my life had other plans for many years. Mostly all good things, like being a good wife, a partner in full time ministry, raising four children, teaching in public and private schools and at church, running my own business, caregiving, legally adopting an adult who had been abused, and you know... all the in-between. You all have similar stories and busy lives.

My first love, Jesus, whom I've been getting to know since I was 7, is my cheerleader for eternity! He is the reason this book should be on anyone's shelf or coffee table or discussed at any Bible study, and the **main** reason I wrote it. My prayer is that it strengthens the faith of those who already know Him, and introduces the idea of a Great, Almighty, and Personal God for those who are not yet acquainted.

My husband of almost forty-five years, Kurt, is my lifelong cheerleader who has always, and still does, believe in me and any endeavor I attempt. He has gone over this work thoroughly, and I trust him; not just because he's my husband, or even because he has a doctorate in Theology and Spiritual Direction, but because he knows the Lord deeply and also wants to offer material that is Biblically sound and worthy of someone's time.

When we purchased the cabin and I began spending weeks in the mountains, I had the perfectly carved-out time to actually pray, think, and write all those life metaphors God began placing on my heart at the tender age of 11 and 12 years old and has continued to show me at the still tender, yet polished around the edges, age of 60+.

The Devotionals and Mirror Moments actually came incredibly easily to me. As you read, you'll see I'm real and often throw myself under the proverbial bus before I've had a chance to learn my lesson. The right Scripture verses took a little longer, and the Communion with the Creator prayers were my own prayers poured out from my heart. The group discussion questions took the longest. I began to feel I wasn't worthy to write out questions that would make sense or a difference to anyone's life, let alone attach Holy Scripture to them. Then...

Then came Monday morning Bible Study! I had ladies who actually wanted to study what I'd written. I'd taught many studies to ladies over several decades, but always from books others had written. I'd taught children with a curriculum I'd penned when the church we had just planted didn't have a dime to offer the kids' ministry, as well as awesome purchased material once the church was able to afford it. These were my comfort zone places. You know, the ones where you know God has gifted you. They came effortlessly.

Getting back to my Monday morning ladies... I'm about to list some precious souls who risked coming to my home and committed to a year of studying with me. And they keep coming! They still come. Blows my mind actually. They have offered encouragement and suggestions and provided me the courage to think others might also find wisdom in these pages. They are a blessing, and their names are listed below.

I also want to thank a dear friend, who wasn't able to come to my study because she teaches during the day, yet has committed to praying for me and my whole family daily for the last several years. Her prayers have been transformational in my life and continue to make a difference in my family's lives as well. Thank you, Billie Hudson.

Along with all these ladies, our adopted daughter, Audrey Joy Oheim, who we legally adopted at the age of 30, researched many of the song suggestions at the end of each devotional. I am incredibly grateful for this, as I feel they have brought a beautiful element into each reading. She was also my guest writer for the devotional, "Wind." Thank you, Audrey Joy. You are a blessing I didn't know God had planned for me.

My precious daddy, Robert "Bob" Pruyn, who, during the completion of this project, reached the century mark of 100 years old. He asks me on a regular basis if I've completed the project. He will be the first to receive a signed copy! I have already read several of the lessons to him, and he always responds with, "You're such a wonderful writer," in his beautiful Southern drawl. He is highlighted in the devotional, "Love Across the Decades".

I also thank my children, who we, my husband and I, have had the honor and privilege of raising and launching into their own successful lives and continue to bless our lives. I love you, Zachary, Grayson, Benjamin, and Hannah. Along with their spouses, they have also been incredibly encouraging to me for the last several years of working on *Lessons From the Mountain*.

And of course, my precious grandchildren:

Julian Wood, who is "wicked smart," always full of questions and keeps me on my toes; London, who is thrilled about beginning pre-K, full of wonder and asks for sleepovers almost daily; Ivan, little towhead, excited about being with Lolli and Padeaux every chance he gets; Luca, precious, and curious about his ever expanding world, and loves his new baby sister; and Norah, the smiliest little one-year-old you could ever meet!

Ladies whom I appreciate and love, and who have attended, and most continue to attend my Bible Study:

Lisa Blake	Kathy Marlett
Debra Bowling	Karly McCutchan
Sandra Davidson	Renee McDaniel
Maggie Dean	Kristin Morales
Linda Dehoyes	April Pierce
Cynthia Dowell	Leesa Penland
Karen Edmondson	Carol Phillips
Chris Fox	Carol Roller
Carolyn Frederich	Diane Saied
Philly Goodman	Lori Schmitt
Gwen Green	Joan Shields
Mary Haygood	Lynn Sherman
Gail Holloway	Mary Sledge
Julie Jasper	Maxine Smith
Glenna Kerr	Linda Thomas
Tammy Laughlin	

There are so many others who have poured into my life over the years.

I wouldn't have been able to accomplish this project, let alone live life to the fullest, without their love and support.

About the Author

Laura Oheim has devoted much of her life to pouring into others—as a partner in ministry alongside her husband, a teacher, and, most of all, as a devoted wife, mother, and grandmother. Married to her husband, Kurt, for forty-four years, she is the proud mother of five grown children and "Lolli" to five grandchildren who keep life lively and full of joy. Her heart for encouragement and faith has shaped her writing, and this book reflects her desire to help others grow closer to God—both personally and in community. Whether used as a devotional or in group study, her words come from years of lived faith, grace, and love.

www.ingramcontent.com/pod-product-compliance
Lightning Source LLC
Chambersburg PA
CBHW021220090426
42740CB00006B/312